"A timely, needed book that helpfully clarifies where wives fit into the great move of the Holy Spirit currently among men. Mary Jenson shows how God is touching whole families, not just men, and how wives can be both used and blessed by God in this movement."

VONETTE BRIGHT
Campus Crusade for Christ

"Many readers will identify with feelings Mary Jenson expresses about being partners with their husbands. Wives will definitely profit by understanding changes taking place in men today. But, most of all, women will find help in clarifying their God-ordained, personal responsibilities by reading *Partners in Promise*."

LINDA WEBER
author of Mom, You're Incredible

"Mary Jenson addresses two critical issues within marital relationships — change and forgiveness. With great tenderness and grace, *Partners in Promise* encourages and assists women in taking the steps to reconcile with their husbands in a way that pleases and glorifies our precious Father God, according to His Word."

CONNIE SCHAEDEL
Promise Reapers

"Men across America are coming home from Promise Keeper rallies committed to being the kind of men their wives can depend upon and their children can look up to. But their success as promise keepers is greatly enhanced by the response of their wives. Mary Jenson has done a tremendous job of showing you how to be an ally and asset to your husband's commitments — a promise builder to your promise keeper."

TIM AND DARCY KIMMEL
Generation Ministries

"Hundreds of thousands of Christian men are filling football stadiums across America wanting to be better husbands and fathers. But how does this work out in practice when they go home to their wives and children? Mary Jenson provides biblical insight and practical wisdom to help you and your husband partner in making your home a place where promises are kept!"

STEVE AND MARY FARRAR
authors of Point Man *and* Choices

"God is at work! Men's hearts are being turned back to their homes all across the land by the hundreds of thousands. As God answers the prayers of women, it is now time to bring Christian families to the point of mutual understanding, genuine love, and a biblical foundation. Mary Jenson's book picks up as men return to their treasured families. She helps women to understand how very powerful, if not pivotal, a woman's responsiveness is to her husband in his spiritual journey."

GARY AND BARB ROSBERG
CrossTrainer Ministries

Partners in Promise

Partners in
Promise

Discovering your role in your husband's spiritual quest

Mary Jenson

MULTNOMAH BOOKS • SISTERS, OREGON

Throughout the book, people's identities, circumstances, and locations
have been altered to protect their privacy.

PARTNERS IN PROMISE
published by Multnomah Books
a part of the Questar publishing family

© 1996 by Mary Jenson

International Standard Book Number: 0-88070-867-0

Cover photo by Paul Figura
Cover design by David Carlson
Edited by Heather Harpham Kopp

Printed in the United States of America

Most Scripture quotations are from:
New American Standard Bible (NASB)
© 1960, 1977 by the Lockman Foundation

Also quoted:
The Holy Bible, New International Version (NIV)
© 1973, 1984 by International Bible Society,
used by permission of Zondervan Publishing House

For information:
QUESTAR PUBLISHERS, INC.
POST OFFICE BOX 1720
SISTERS, OREGON 97759

96 97 98 99 00 01 02 03 — 10 9 8 7 6 5 4 3 2 1

To Ron,
whose character, stability, and love for me
make it hard to remember that God is God, and
he's just my husband.

And to Matt and Molly,
who've proven Psalm 112:1–2 —
"Blessed is the man who fears the LORD....
His children will be mighty in the land" (NIV).

C O N T E N T S

F O R E W O R D

Promises, changes, adjustments, and progress. That's what my dear friend Mary Jenson has written about in this, her debut into the world of publishing. And what a wonderful beginning it is. Mary has always been an engaging, informative, personally honest letter writer. Her book is no exception.

Neither of us can remember when we met. But we both clearly remember the summer thirteen years ago when Dennis and I arrived in Ft. Collins, Colorado, with the second of our five children, Benjamin, recovering from chicken pox. Four long weeks later all the Rainey children had succumbed, and it was Matt and Molly Jenson's turn to develop the tell-tale rash.

Both families had journeyed to Ft. Collins because Mary's husband, Ron, and my husband, Dennis, had been invited to teach at the Institute of Biblical Studies for Campus Crusade for Christ. And so began a collection of summer adventures that spanned more than a decade. Every year in early June, I would pack up our ever-increasing family (the first year we had only three) with all the paraphernalia that young children and babies require, and we would drive in our bulging van to Ft. Collins. There we would live for two months in a small, sparsely furnished, two-bedroom apartment. Ron and Mary did the same.

Those apartments became sort of a Christian commune. We often left our doors open and talked across the hall. We freely borrowed from one another, and our children all played together. They roller-skated up and down the halls. They went to child-care together. They shared toys and peanut butter sandwiches and germs. In the evenings, we watched our children ride their big-wheels or jump rope in the courtyard. Many nights, after the kids were asleep, we'd play cards or hire a college student to baby-sit while all four adults escaped to a movie. Usually, however, the Jensons and the Raineys would just sit and visit.

Sounds idyllic, doesn't it? In many ways it was. Mary and I "clicked" with one another. Maybe it was our mutual love for children, books, and decorating. She became one of those friends that "wears well." I found what you will discover in her book — Mary is a real person. She is a great mother and an excellent wife. When you live as close as we did over the years, you find out quickly if a marriage is truly authentic. Mary's is!

She knows firsthand about change. Her husband, like mine, loves change. Mary has devoted an entire chapter to the ramifications of change on both husband and wife. As I read it, I underlined and highlighted several sections, which I read to Dennis to further our understanding of each other. And then, not three hours later, we found ourselves in the middle of a serious (from my perspective) miscommunication, which necessitated a change for me. It was one of those "he thought he had told me" kinds of misunderstandings. It took a fair amount of time, but thanks to what I'd just read in this book, we talked it through.

You'll find that Mary's book is full of principles you will be able to apply immediately to your marriage. Dennis and I are both thrilled she's used her talent with words to write a book that will bring hope and encouragement for your marriage. Listen to the advice she's collected. Follow her example. See what the Lord will do for you.

It is my prayer that God will richly bless you and your husband and your children as you read this book. May you courageously choose to believe the promises of God regarding your marriage and family. He never breaks His promises as do we fallible humans. May you grant and receive forgiveness when you fail, never giving up but continuing to grow. And may you become an example to others. Our world is desperate for the encouragement of those who are on the road to success and are conscious of the fact they haven't arrived.

To Mary, Dennis and I say a wholehearted, "Well done." And to all the Jensons from the eight of us, we love you.

BARBARA RAINEY
Wife and mother of six
Cofounder of FamilyLife Ministries

ACKNOWLEDGMENTS

I thought I knew what an editor was, until I met Heather Harpham Kopp. Questar took a chance on me; it wasn't much of a risk because they yoked me with Heather, and no one can fail with her on the team. We'd probably have been finished faster if we hadn't become such good friends.

Thanks also to my researcher/friend Debbie Hedstrom, who has an ability "which passes my understanding" to zero in on the important stuff.

Thanks to Laurie Arabe, Connie Arthur, Nancy Bayless, Vicki Bentley, Linda Cash, Jennie Gillespie, Heather Johnston, Gayle Linn, Elaine Minamide, Elaine Minton, Jan Scholes, and Claire West. All these women read, critiqued, discussed, and/or contributed to this book in numerous ways. And thanks to the many other men and women whose stories are in or behind these pages. You're the partners in promise.

And finally, thanks to Dennis and Barbara Rainey — who got me into this.

By all the laws both of logic and simple arithmetic, to give yourself away in love to another would seem to mean that you end up with less of yourself left than you had to begin with. But the miracle is that just the reverse is true, logic and arithmetic go hang. To give yourself away in love to somebody else — as a man and a woman give themselves away to each other at a wedding — is to become for the first time yourself fully. To live not just for yourself alone anymore but for another self, to whom you swear to be true, is to come fully alive. Things needn't have been that way as far as we know, but that is the way things are, that is the way life is, and if you and I are inclined to have any doubts about it, we can always put it to the test. The test, needless to say, is our lives themselves.

DR. FREDERICK BUECHNER

Behold the Stadium

Behold the stadium. The grass is deep green and flawlessly edged. The baselines are raked smooth and straight as rulers. Nothing disturbs this scene...except for dozens of white paper airplanes nose-diving onto the field and bright-colored beach balls ricocheting from one section of seats to another. In the stands thousands of half-hoarse men, many wearing T-shirts that say "Real Men Sing Real Loud," bellow out a song that shakes the ground.

It wasn't exactly the picture I had expected — this men-only Promise Keepers' mega-rally, nearly identical to dozens of others being held each year around the country.

So what am I, a woman, doing here? Besides struggling to locate just *one* ladies' room that hasn't been appropriated by the men, I'm trying to get the inside scoop for us wives back at home. What really goes on at these and other men's revivals? What are so many men excited about? And most importantly, what kinds of changes can women in the other stadium — the *home* field — expect as a result?

A spiritual reawakening among men is sweeping the country. From Promise Keepers (PK) to numerous other national men's ministries and church revivals, the evidence is in: God is moving powerfully among men.

Profound changes are happening as a result. Men are taking back their God-given responsibilities and keeping their promises: to honor commitments made to their wives, to participate actively in the raising of their children, to grow in their spiritual lives, to become involved in their churches, to erase racial barriers.

Some groups, such as PK, are so large that they have drawn attention from the secular media. And the impact of these groups, observers are quick to point out, isn't limited to men. Everyone stands to be affected — wives in particular. Some wives are nervous about the changes. Many others are excited, wanting to become partners in the promises their husbands are making.

So why would wives need a book in response to their husbands' spiritual growth? Perhaps because coping with any kind of change is hard. And if your husband is changing, because you are one with him, you will likely be making adjustments of your own in response.

The Fields of Change

Why is change so hard? Even in less-than-healthy situations, sameness often feels a lot more comfortable than change. That's because change is about loss of control. Allowing our husbands to move forward could involve reassessing the way they relate to our kids, releasing our own need to determine every outcome, and letting our husbands make informed decisions regarding finances (or even the route to the movie theater).

Although my husband and I have been married twenty-six years, I still find it unsettling for him to change in any way. Ron's a good guy, easy to live with. If I could wean him from the TV remote control and keep him from pruning my bougainvillea, I wouldn't change another thing. I've simply become accustomed to his way of doing things. I *trust* him to stay the same. But he doesn't!

Part of our experience with change has been in the spiritual side of our lives. For many years Ron and I struggled to pray together. Ron would suggest one time; I'd prefer another. He'd set aside ten minutes; I'd want an hour. Finally he quit trying, and I let him.

Several years ago Ron tried something new. One day we slipped on our Reeboks for a long stroll in the neighborhood. It was a great day for walking, foggy and cool. The sounds of morning were shrouded, lacking their usual sharp ping. Kids were arriving at the school behind our house, and even the neon colors of their backpacks looked muted in the fog. Fog-water dripped from my bangs.

And then Ron began to pray out loud. "Father, thank you for this walk Mary and I get to have. And for this beautiful place we live in."

Don't ask me why, but somewhere inside I pulled away. I let this small change in our routine walks drop a curtain between us. I stayed silent, resisting my husband's attempts to make us a team in this spiritual area. I kept my eyes on the dirt at my feet, letting him pray but definitely not "agreeing in prayer."

Would your husband initiate prayer again if you responded as I did? Maybe it was just the shift in the familiar; maybe it was pure competition or stubbornness. But as human as my response was, it further discouraged Ron's spiritual leadership in our home.

When two people are so close, and one begins to change, even in small ways, it affects the other person. Even if some of the results are point-by-point identical to our prayers, new ways of doing things often produce discomfort. But our response to those changes is key to long-term growth.

Looking back over my journal entry for April 21, 1995, I found this admission:

*Had a rough day yesterday. Computer problems and disappointment
with Ron. It pointed out to me just how much I expect Ron to toe my
line, to always be the same. If anything slips, it throws me for a loop
and I blow it. I am such a child — pouting, slamming things, giving
myself room but not him.*

The point is that when Ron moves a new direction, good or bad, I have
to adjust somewhere too. I have to remember that change is *healthy*. It sig-
nifies growth and movement and learning. It makes life positive and vibrant.
Our husbands' changes are usually good for them *and* us. And if we want to
be partners in promise with them, we must choose our responses carefully.

Cheering and Jeering

One might imagine that every wife whose husband is intent on improving
himself would be ecstatic. What wife wouldn't want her husband to be more
devoted to her and the children? More committed to God? It does seem that
the majority of women love what's happening. In fact, many wives are
encouraging their husbands to attend various Christian men's events.

"Tom went to Promise Keepers with fifteen guys from his church, and I
noticed a huge change in him right away," Karen told me. "One important
thing PK says is to out-serve your wives, to be a role model of servanthood
for your family." Karen really needed this extra help from Tom as she was
working full-time *and* going to school *and* mothering two children.

"One night I casually asked him if he'd get me a cup of coffee," says
Karen. "He said, 'Not right now, Honey; I'm in the middle of something.'
Several minutes went by, and the next thing I knew, Tom had left his proj-
ect, gone downstairs, and made me a cup of coffee, just the way I like it. As
he set it in front of me, he said, 'Sorry, Karen. I want to serve you as often as
I can.' I was very impressed!"

Debbie, a wife and mother of two boys in southern California, was
delighted when her husband returned from a large men's rally in Los

Angeles. "It made Scott more sensitive to my needs," she said. "He listens a lot better, and he's willing to do small things that matter to me, such as give me a backrub or watch the kids while I go out."

But this is not the scene in every household, and change isn't always so welcome. "I knew how much of a change Christ made in my life," Wendy said, "and that Justin would be facing a similar dramatic change. But I expected it to draw us closer together and give us more of a common bond. When he became so close to the men in the church, and yet didn't know how to communicate his changed heart and outlook back to me, I felt really shut out."

When a wife is less than enthusiastic, it doesn't necessarily mean that her husband is doing it all wrong or that she doesn't welcome his attempts to grow. It means that change can be threatening, even when it's aimed at bettering things. And if growth in our husbands means we need to change the way we do things, it's no wonder some women bristle as much as they rejoice.

Many factors play into a wife's response. The husband and wife's personal history as a couple plays a big role, as well as the wife's own life-experience, personality, and spiritual maturity. Sometimes a negative reaction relates back to broken promises or disappointed expectations in a marriage. Why should she get her hopes up again?

Bitter disappointment may have motivated the unknown party who drafted this banner: "Men do not own women and children." This message streamed behind a tiny plane flying above the seventy-two thousand promise keepers who packed the Detroit Silverdome in March 1995. Clearly the banner was intended to directly challenge the PK teachings about the need for male leadership in the home.

Ironically the true aim of the PK teaching is that men lead their homes by *serving their wives and children and sacrificing for them.*

Admittedly there are sensitive issues within the men's movement. No wonder men at the large Promise Keepers' events are warned that they'll go home to one of these three responses from their wives:

- Excitement — "Oh, honey, I've been waiting and praying for this for such a long time!"
- Skepticism — "Well, I'm glad the weekend was so motivating. We'll see what happens."
- Resistance — "We're doing fine just the way things are. *I* don't plan to change, anyway."

The Heart of a Partner

I stepped down from the platform after delivering two hour-long lectures on being a wife and mother. An attractive woman, comfortably dressed in jeans and a T-shirt, approached me with a desperate look in her eyes. Mother of four and married over twenty years, she explained that she and her husband were here at a FamilyLife Marriage Conference in a last-ditch attempt to resurrect some feelings for each other and save their marriage.

"Good for them," I thought to myself. "I bet they've learned a lot. I wonder what she thought of what I had to say? If they're here together, I imagine we can call this marriage successfully saved and add it to the statistics. How fun that I get to hear the story!"

That's not what happened. Alternately rubbing her hands and crossing her arms, she laid down the history of their marriage. No infidelity, drugs, or alcohol. Just lots of fighting for twenty years. "I want out of this," she said.

"What's your husband feeling right now?" I asked.

"I don't know; we haven't talked much this weekend."

"You haven't? Not even on the date night?"

"No."

I was stymied. This couple had been through most of the conference and evidently had sat stony faced during all the interaction times built into the schedule. "What do you think is the biggest obstacle you two are facing?" I asked.

"I think *he's* the problem. He's so stubborn; he won't budge on anything. I was surprised he even wanted to come to this conference. He thinks something is going to change now, like just being here is enough!"

"What about you? What do you think your role is in this?"

"I'm not going to take any steps until he does."

By the time I talked to this woman, the conference was nearly over. She'd heard all she needed to hear, and she hadn't heard a thing. Their mutual stubbornness appeared to be the death of hope for them.

It requires nerve to take the first step in a relationship, and just as much nerve to respond to it. Many men are coming home jazzed up to take that step. Will we wives be ready to become partners, to meet them halfway — or more?

What part will you play? How can you help your husband's being "jazzed up" evolve into something more lasting? The answers aren't always easy or simple, but you *can* discover your role in your husband's spiritual quest.

Is This Book for You?

Because I can't address every situation, I've written with these assumptions in mind:

1. You're interested in how to support and cheer on your changing husband — without having your efforts backfire.
2. You have a positive attitude toward marriage in general and your marriage in particular.
3. You recognize that you may need to make some changes as well.

I've talked with many women and quite a few men about these issues. The responses to what's happening in the Christian men's movement were as varied as the personalities and situations of the wives I asked. Here are some of the comments I heard:

- "I like the changes I'm seeing. But how can they last?"
- "I'm feeling left out of things. Why can't I be included?"
- "He's so different now. I'd never want the old 'him' back."
- "He says he's changing, but I can't see it."
- "Is this just going to be a flash-in-the-pan sort of thing?"
- "Things started out great, but now he's back to being the same old guy as before."
- "My husband says he wants to be a leader in our home. What does that mean for me?"
- "He's got all these new buddies. I feel like they're getting more from him than I am."
- "Should I leave him alone or spur him on?"
- "How do I help *motivate* him without *manipulating* him?"

Do any of these issues ring a bell? If so, you're reading the right book. My own husband is deeply involved in several men's groups. I'd like to pass on to you, wife to wife, what I'm learning on this journey. Woman to woman is the best place for us to start because we all, in our various stages of marriage, can ask these same two questions: How can we continue to focus on our own growth while our husbands are focusing on theirs? And how can we speed our husbands *on their way* — without getting *in their way*?

Help Is on the Way?

This is a book about helping, but not in the usual sense. It won't help you revamp your husband's walk with God or get him away from the TV. We *will* explore the true meaning of help, which often looks like just the opposite. In fact, to enhance your husband's growth — to bless it and not hinder it — may at times mean doing nothing.

I'm convinced that women must approach this men's movement with respect — it's their movement, after all. If we waltz in with grandiose plans to get involved or determine the outcome, we could end up hindering what God is doing or planning.

However, some aspects of our partnership *are* active. We're married to these guys. We share space with them, and toothpaste, and sheets. If we sit back with our hands folded and refuse to encourage when encouragement is needed, we're really *in the way*. There are things we can do and attitudes we can hold that will help us prepare for the changes our men are bringing home.

These are some of the things we'll talk about in the pages to come:
- what our men are *really* hearing and feeling
- how to deal with change
- what change means on a day-to-day basis
- how to honor our husbands
- how to encourage without pressuring
- how to respond if men aren't making the changes we want
- what part forgiveness and acceptance play in change
- how the roles of leadership play out in a Christian family
- how friends are a crucial support during change
- how change benefits your family and the community
- how your own growth fits into the picture

A Promise to Reap

Outnumbered fifty thousand to one, Connie Schaedel stepped up to the Promise Keepers microphone in Anaheim, California. It was a Saturday afternoon. She spoke about her husband, Bud. The stadium grew very quiet.

Bud's one of those guys, she explained, who started out being a good husband and father. On the outside, things looked great. But when Promise Keepers put the challenge of godliness before him, he knew in his heart that he was ready for change. After his first conference, Connie saw the difference and stood back to watch God take this good man and make him better.

When the next conference came around, Bud invited over two hundred fifty men from his church. But then, tragically, two weeks before the Anaheim conference, Bud died. One of his final requests to Connie was that his registration be handed over to his non-Christian son-in-law in the hopes that God would begin a work in this young man's life.

His wish and his prayer were granted. Andy attended the conference and responded to what God was saying to him. "I wasn't much of a church-going guy," Andy says. "Certainly not on a regular basis. I'd seen a lot of double standards when I was growing up, and they'd left me rather skeptical. I told my father-in-law I'd go out of respect for him, but that was all.

"When I went to Promise Keepers, I had an idea of what it'd be like. But I'd given no thought to the actual subject matter or the huge numbers of men that would attend. Most of all, I didn't expect any changes in my life. It's a good thing I went with an open mind because it was overwhelming!"

Connie charged her rapt audience to take up the same gauntlet that Bud had carried, and to accept the challenge to follow God with whole hearts. Most of them did. And now lots of their wives are calling Connie and asking, "Now what do I do?"

Maybe you are asking the same question. Connie's short answer to wives is this: Become a *promise reaper*[1] — make the most of the work God is doing in your husband. You're the lucky beneficiary! Praise God and give Him the glory, as well as your heartaches and questions.

In the next chapter we'll learn more about this so-called revival. Where's it coming from? What are the secrets wives don't know? We'll hear from husbands, as well as from leaders in the Christian men's movement. You might be surprised by what these men think, and what *they* think *we* think!

Getting Back to the Word

I hope you'll take advantage of these study sections at the end of each chapter. Each study offers questions that are designed to be answered in a group setting but can also be used alone. The questions are not meant to be inclusive, nor are they meant to limit your thoughts or discussions. Each session also includes Private Consideration — questions intended solely for your private contemplation or response.

We dare not measure the Truth by our experiences, but our experiences by the Truth. The following verses remind us that the Bible is able to have an influence on our lives like no other words.

2 Timothy 3:16 — *"All Scripture is inspired by God and profitable for teaching, for reproof, for correction, for training in righteousness."*

Hebrews 4:12 — *"For the word of God is living and active and sharper than any two-edged sword, and piercing as far as the division of soul and spirit, of both joints and marrow, and able to judge the thoughts and intentions of the heart."*

Promising Conversations

> Philippians 1:6 — *"For I am confident of this very thing, that He who began a good work in you will perfect it until the day of Christ Jesus."*

> Philippians 2:12–13 — *"So then, my beloved, just as you have always obeyed…work out your salvation with fear and trembling; for it is God who is at work in you, both to will and to work for His good pleasure."*

1. What's happening in your marriage that is motivating you to read this book?

2. Write down five words or phrases that describe the ideal Christian marriage.

3. What are/were the strong/weak points of your parents' marriage? How has their marriage influenced yours?

4. How interested are you in supporting your husband's growth?

5. Describe your attitude toward your marriage.

6. What changes are you facing aside from your husband's changes?

Private Consideration

1. Stop and think about your husband's life. You know him better than anyone else does. What are the toughest areas he's facing? Of those tough areas, which one(s) will you commit to pray for, encourage, support?

2. What are some of the areas in his life and character that are a continual blessing to you? Does he know this?

For a person is the single most limitless entity in creation, and if there is anything that is even more unlimited and unrestrained in its possibilities than is a person, then it is two people together.

MIKE MASON

Trading Footballs for Faith

Michael had been a Christian for eight years when he attended his first men's gathering. He didn't go into it blindly, but once there he said, "My feelings were enormous. I didn't believe all the reports. There really were fifty-five thousand men! These were the same kinds of guys I'd competed with for clients — and they all loved God. It was so healing for me personally.

"I'd be waiting to use the phone and find myself talking with total strangers about stuff I've never talked about before. All of a sudden I didn't feel so alone. And I wasn't even aware that I had felt alone."

Michael's story is just one of the thousands of positive reports from the Christian men's movement. You may have noticed that most men haven't actually traded in their footballs or their TVs — they're just watching in small groups now. In fact, a broad range of groups has sprung up in order to meet the huge demand for men's gatherings.

How did it all get started, and why? Curious wives want to know — and understand.

Naturally if you and I can learn more about what's motivating our husbands — what they're really learning and feeling — chances are we'll be better equipped to respond to the changes they're going through. We'll also be better equipped to address our own questions, fears, and misconceptions.

In the Company of Men

I was in the company of more men than I'd ever seen in one place before. Armed with a VIP pass, I was permitted to enter the most sacrosanct place in the Oakland Coliseum — the Raiders' locker room. I was also permitted to join the forty-nine thousand men and handful of women for a Promise Keepers' rally.

For me, the event began before I arrived. While walking to the Bay Area Rapid Transit (BART), I passed a herd of cowboys with big hats on their heads and big boots on their feet. They carried thick Bibles tucked under their arms like baby calves. They explained that they were on their way to get a good seat for the 7:00 P.M. opening of the conference — at 3:30 in the afternoon!

I rode the BART with these and many, many other men. I felt surprisingly safe, welcome, and secure — and conducted a few interviews on the way. I heard a lot of stories like this one:

"A bunch of guys from my church are here together," explained a tall, bearded man with kind, dark eyes. "We went to a rally in Los Angeles in June and had a great time. A friend's marriage was on the ropes, and he was planning to leave his wife. We kept telling him, 'Don't leave. Don't leave. Pray. God can fix things.' After he heard all the messages and we were ready to leave, twelve of us prayed for him.

"Then this brother said, 'I'm glad I came because now I know how to treat my wife.' Immediately after Promise Keepers they went on a second honeymoon."

With that and other testimonies under my hat, I walked expectantly into the stadium, trying not to feel self-conscious about my gender. Making my way through this sea of testosterone-under-control, I slipped gratefully into my seat. As the evening got started, I leaned forward to get the full effect, closed my eyes to the individual faces, and sharpened my hearing.

In the back of my memory was the high-pitched hum of women's voices, familiar from countless retreats. But this sound was nothing like that. The murmuring resonated like the bass instruments of an orchestra tuning up before a concert. And when the combined voices of all those men came together to sing the first of many songs, the harmony, depth, and richness of the music astounded me.

I listened and took notes during most sessions, which were laid out in light of, but not exactly like, the seven Promise Keepers' promises. Since this is one of the most visible men's ministries, and my husband has been deeply involved in it, I was surprised to realize I didn't actually know what the seven promises are! Do you?

The Seven Promises of a Promise Keeper

1. A Promise Keeper is committed to honoring Jesus Christ through worship, prayer, and obedience to His Word, in the power of the Holy Spirit.
2. A Promise Keeper is committed to pursuing vital relationships with a few other men, understanding that he needs brothers to help him keep his promises.
3. A Promise Keeper is committed to practicing spiritual, moral, ethical, and sexual purity.
4. A Promise Keeper is committed to building strong marriages and families through love, protection, and biblical values.

5. A Promise Keeper is committed to supporting the mission of the church by honoring and praying for his pastor and by actively giving his time and resources.

6. A Promise Keeper is committed to reaching beyond any racial and denominational barriers to demonstrate the power of biblical unity.

7. A Promise Keeper is committed to influencing his world, being obedient to the Great Commandment (see Mark 12:30–31) and the Great Commission (see Matthew 28:19–20).

The speakers at the Oakland PK rally came from different cities, denominations, businesses, or ministries. The differences in dress, accents, ethnicity, and occupation testified that this was indeed a diverse gathering. All were men, except for a ten-minute greeting Saturday afternoon from Holly Phillips, wife of PK president, Randy Phillips. Here are the highlights of what I heard:

Pastor Jack Hayford asked the men to remove their shoes because they were on holy ground. "Something's flaming across this nation," he said. "Thousands of guys are turning aside to hear God. And He's recognizing this turning."

Randy Phillips warned the men against mediocrity with a story from 2 Kings 13 about Elisha and Joash.

Dallas Seminary professor Howard Hendricks left the crowd with this phrase: "Dusty Bibles always lead to dirty lives."

Speaker Ed Cole admonished the men to recognize their wives as joint heirs and partners, saying, "A joint heir shouldn't have to beg for money like a slave."

Speaker Wellington Boone focused on racial reconciliation with his reminder that "being a slave to God means being a slave to His purposes."

Coach Bill McCartney, founder of Promise Keepers, closed the conference with this powerful statement: "All you need to do is look into a wife's eyes to see a man's character."

These glimpses of many of the speakers for this conference confirmed a comment Michael made to me. "This is *for* women," he said, "but not about them." This addresses the number one question from wives: Are we losing something here, or gaining? Can men gather in such massive numbers and not begin to feel their "male power" over women even more keenly?

In fact, the most powerful impression I came away with was that of being safely immersed in a sea of men of every ilk — bald, hairy, short, tall, trim, not, black, white, brown, old, young. I didn't have one moment of concern for my welfare or notice an ounce of disrespect. Nowhere did I hear the message that women are not equal to men or that we're less capable or less important.

This honoring attitude appeared to carry over to women outside the conference as well. Women working the concessions commented on the patience of their customers. My hotel restaurant waitress, in her thick accent, commented on the graciousness of the men staying in our hotel. "It's been so busy," she said. "But everyone is so nice, it doesn't matter."

From the Mouths of Men

So what's driving all these men to the dozens of men-focused ministries? And what are they exactly? The most visible of men's ministries is Promise Keepers, which overtakes whole coliseums in various cities around the country. Other arms of the men's movement, such as The National Center for Fathering, Man's Authentic Nature (MAN), CrossTrainers, Men's Leadership Ministries, Generation Ministries, and many others, have grown up to meet men's needs.

While maintaining unique specifics, these ministries and many others like them overlap in several areas. They all address the needs of men to grow spiritually and relationally. And they agree on several points: The nation is in turmoil, and too many men have abdicated leadership of the family and have forsaken the pursuit of godly manhood, but God is moving.

I thought it would be helpful to talk candidly with several of the leaders of these ministries, all of whom are also authors. The following is an interview with Tim Kimmel (Generation Ministries), Steve Farrar (Men's Leadership Ministries), Gary Rosberg (CrossTrainers and a marriage and family counselor), and my husband, Ron (High Ground).

All four of these men interact with Christian groups of men, small and large, in their day-to-day work. I invaded a lunch meeting to ask them some of the questions that have puzzled me most.

"What is behind the Christian men's movement?"

STEVE: *There's a place on the Niagara River that's fairly calm and placid. But if you go past that point, you're going over the falls. I think America has passed the point of no return, morally. And I think there's no hope left, unless God does something along the lines of the Great Awakening.*

However, a number of men are sensing something's deeply wrong, and they're being awakened by the Spirit of God to the critical role they play. As the nation deteriorates, God's going back to his game plan, which is men leading the family and men leading the church.

TIM: *I think that God is finally answering the prayers of all the women. They've been praying for about fifty years, "Get in my husband's face, and get him back in the cause." And so God says, "Okay." And the Spirit is now moving among men.*

STEVE: *Personally, I think America's under judgment. Martin Lloyd-Jones says that the key element in revival, from a human perspective, is desperation. God's people must be desperate. We're not there yet, but I think when persecution comes, we'll be there. And I think it's coming.*

GARY: *The other thing I've seen is that things are becoming increasingly black-and-white. Even in the last three years the gray is beginning to diminish, and people are beginning to take stands, one way or the other. I think we're going to look less and less like the world.*

"What part, if any, does the feminist movement play?"

TIM: *I don't know whether the women's movement is a cause as much as it's a symptom. I'm playing with words here. I think if you emasculate men, they will not survive. Somewhere a major threat stirs up courage in people. People are realizing if we don't do something, it's going down. When you can look in your own lifetime and see a nation on a nosedive, it makes you ask where it's going to be ten years from now.*

RON: *Men are reacting to a loss of identity, to the whole issue of leadership and where they fit. I think guys just don't know what it means to be a man.*

STEVE: *They're confused.*

"Is there a stereotype for the man involved in this movement?"

STEVE: *No — I think the world is trying to stereotype them.*

RON: *You've got every color, every denomination, CEOs, bikers. It is, however, biased the way the body of Christ is, in terms of stronger marriages than the average in society.*

"What, if anything, would surprise wives about what happens at these meetings?"

GARY: *Watching men truly enjoy being active in their worship and fellowship with other men.*

RON: *The affection, the level of emotion, touching.*

STEVE: *I think a lot of women would be upset at what they see, and jealous, thinking, "Why can't he ever do that with me?"*

"How do men gain strength from each other? How do these meetings help men overcome depression, anxiety, stress, apathy, identity problems?"

GARY: *Just walking in the stadium starts the process. You walk in and you think, "All these guys are here because they want to experience God, strengthen relationships, families."*

RON: *Finding that they're not alone has been a great comfort.*

TIM: *But these meetings don't help unless there's a level of vulnerability or transparency there. When CrossTrainers started in our city, everybody had their masks on, their guards up. But little by little as the testimonies came, men realized it was safe to be transparent there.*

"Is there a great difference between the impact of the large meetings/conferences and small groups?"

TIM: *Each serves a different purpose. The pep rally gives them that sense that "I'm not alone, and not only am I not alone, but I am part of a very large group of people here who are serious about what they're doing."*

When you go to PK, it feels like the guys have been holding their ground in a war zone, and you're bivouacked out there. You've got your little machine gun, and you've been taking it. But then you hear that fresh troops are on the way. You get there and see that, yea, you've got help. It makes you more courageous.

GARY: *I think it's the difference between the honeymoon and the marriage. The wedding and honeymoon are great; that's Promise Keepers. But as soon as they get home on Saturday night the marriage begins. And then they need long-term accountability, support, friendship. That's the small groups.*

"How important to you is the aspect of being with only men? How would it change things if women were allowed in?"

STEVE: *How would it change things at a women's retreat if they let men in? Goes both ways. Some things are better communicated and experienced when you have women or men only.*

RON: *We found even in the big PK events when you have just men there, they're free to worship. But if even one woman comes in to speak, guys start to close down. Traditionally the church, though led by men, has catered to women in the Bible studies, the kinds of questions that are asked, materials that have been developed. When a man becomes part of a male context, he feels a real freedom to open up.*

TIM: *In the book* We Were Soldiers Once and Young, *there's a paragraph about the love men develop for each other in a war situation. The author says it's different than the love a man has for his wife. He'll have a deep love for her but a different type of love for a fellow soldier. When the only hope you have is the guy on either side of you, and you're depending on each other to stay alive — there's something about that feeling.*

There's just a difference in the way guys are. To throw a woman in the middle of that is to wreck a dynamic. Certain things are all right for just men to do and just women to do.

At my Few Good Men conference I asked the question, "Is it easier to lie to your wife or to a real close male friend?" It's interesting that the numbers tend to side with "It's easier to lie to my wife." And the reason is because I have so much to lose if I tell her the truth. She could punish me indefinitely for it.

The difference with the man is that he's a friend, and he's not going to write me off just because I was a jerk. He's not going to punish me, and he's not going to feel like there's something basically unusual about the fact I'm a jerk.

Men can go outside a bar, beat each other up, come back in, and buy each other a drink. We get it all out of our system. Women aren't wired that way.

"In what areas do men most want to change, and why?"

GARY: *I think they want to assume the role God has prescribed for them as leaders. When guys walk out of that stadium, they're thinking, "I want to go home and lead." That's where the gap is — between the motivation and the know-how. They want to lead, but they don't have the plan.*

RON: *They want to change the roles they're living in — be better husbands and dads. They want to get their self-respect back. But they're not sure how it will be received at home.*

GARY: *The bus trips back from PK are the most tender, honest, sweet times. Then these guys get off the bus, and that's where things happen — a sociological phenomenon. Some wives run to embrace them; other wives sit back.*

It's like when Barb and I go on vacation. About five minutes in the car and we start talking. And while we're away, we relax. But as soon as we get back into the car to head home to "reality," my tension level escalates.

That's what happens with these guys. They get caught off guard. They're here hugging and crying and screaming and laughing , but then usually Saturday afternoon they start thinking, "Yeah, but Sally's waiting for me, and I have to get home. And I'm a mediocre guy, and I don't know my kids very well."

Ouch. What sobering thoughts! It's so easy to forget that a husband who isn't cutting it probably knows it. And he hurts. We have such great potential as wives to help or hinder, to crush or encourage growth in our husbands. Though we don't have total control, we can't hear this interview and still think we have no effect.

We'll hear a bit more of this interview in the next chapter, but we can make some observations at this point about the Christian men's movement:

- The men's movement is a work of God first of all, not merely a reaction to feminism or other forces.
- The movement is meeting the deep needs for fellowship that men have felt, or not felt, for years.
- The goals of the leadership are shaped by the Bible, not by egos.
- Women are not denigrated in these meetings.
- Not just one kind of guy goes to these meetings — the men cross all boundaries of profession, race, and class.
- It's important to men that women respect the movement's exclusivity to men.
- The majority of men who attend are seeking a sincere renewal of faith and commitment — and many fear that they will fail at home.

In the next chapter we'll focus on the women's side of the men's movement. Are the changes our husbands are making the same ones we hope for at home? If we love the changes, how can we partner with our men to help the promises last? And by the way, how do you greet a guy who's coming home on a bus with revival under one arm — and a football still under the other?

Promising Conversations

Hebrews 10:23–25 — *"Let us hold fast the confession of our hope without wavering, for He who promised is faithful; and let us consider how to stimulate one another to love and good deeds, not forsaking our own assembling together, as is the habit of some, but encouraging one another; and all the more, as you see the day drawing near."*

1. Paraphrase these verses as if they had been written specifically to you. How, then, would you apply these verses to your role in your husband's growth?

In chapter two we sat in on an interview with a group of leaders in the men's movement. From that interview and others we learned that men are being encouraged to serve their wives, not step on them.

2. Are you seeing evidence of this?

3. What has attending Promise Keepers or similar men's ministries done for your husband?

4. How do you feel about the changes you're seeing in your husband?

Private Consideration

Think carefully through your marriage. Looking at your paraphrase of Hebrews 10:23–25, write down three truths to hold on to, act upon, memorize, or meditate on.

A good relationship has a pattern like a dance and is built on some of the same rules. The partners do not need to hold on tightly, because they move confidently in the same pattern, intricate but gay and swift and free, like a country dance of Mozart's.... There is no place here for the possessive clutch, the clinging arm...because they know they are partners moving to the same rhythm, creating a pattern together, and being invisibly nourished by it.

ANNE MORROW LINDBERGH

From Where a Wife Stands

Your husband has just arrived home after a weekend at a Christian men's gathering in another town. You step out of your car, prepared on the outside to meet him. He stumbles off a church bus, weary, unshaven, smiling shyly. He's just had a pep talk the likes of which he's never heard before. He's fired up for something. He's never seemed so ready to make changes. The question is, are you ready?

Charlie and Madeleine live in St. Louis with their six-year-old son, Alex. He happens to have Attention Deficit Disorder (ADD). Several years ago Alex's energy and wild behavior were complicating every area of their lives — so much so that Charlie began to work excessive hours as a way to escape. "He either stayed late at work," Madeleine says, "or he would go golfing or fishing."

This left Madeleine mostly alone with the burden of caring for their son. Charlie's own increasing depression about Alex compounded Madeleine's loneliness. "One day he came home from a night out with friends, and I was so ticked off.... Alex had been screaming in his room for an hour, kicking the walls and yelling that he hated me. I was ready to pack my bags."

Fortunately Charlie agreed to try harder. Soon after, he attended a men's weekend retreat through their church. There he gained the courage to really listen to Madeleine. When he got home, he asked her to explain what she'd been going through as virtually the sole parent of this troubled child. "Boy, did I let it blow!" says Madeleine.

But to her relief, Charlie didn't leave. "He didn't even retreat into his customary depression," she says. "He apologized."

A year after taking this first step, Charlie attended another men's group. This time, it was a rally. "Charlie came home a new person," Madeleine said through tears that made her words almost unintelligible. "He's so totally different. The smallest thing used to send him into a depression, and I'd lose him for the weekend. Now he runs through the door to give me a hug."

Charlie has made a lot of the personal changes Madeleine dreamed of — and needed. Many marriages are doing an about-face because of the willingness of husbands — and wives — to face their inadequacies and take some steps of growth. But the first step is not always the last, and not every man turns into Prince Charlie.

Maybe you can relate to Madeleine. Or, maybe you will relate better to Wendy and Evan, a fictional but typical couple.

Wendy and Evan have been married six years and have several small children. Evan is a salesman, traveling 40 percent of his time; Wendy is a trained computer programmer, with her career on hold. Evan is gone so much that Wendy often feels like a single parent, handling the finances, disciplining the kids, calling repairmen, and overseeing pretty much the entire household.

Then, one weekend in the spring, with Wendy's encouragement, Evan attends a CrossTrainer conference at a nearby hotel. He appreciates the teaching, but what really hits home is that he needs to be a better overseer of his home and family. So he goes home, intending to make a few changes.

Wendy's thrilled, initially, when Evan offers to take on the job of paying bills for a time. But then he lets a few bills pile up. Wendy has always prided herself on avoiding interest payments on their credit cards. Next, Evan cuts his travel time down so he can lead family devotions two Fridays a month. Unfortunately, Wendy had grown used to setting aside those Friday nights for herself.

Wendy's happy for Evan, but she's beginning to wonder what she got herself into.

Clashing Views

What is Wendy getting into? Change is definitely in the air, and Evan is motivated by his deep desire to do something right for the first time in a long time. Just because it's not exactly what Wendy pictured doesn't mean it's not good. But being a partner in promise will obviously involve some compromising and adjusting for Wendy.

She and Madeleine represent just two types of feedback women are offering to the men's movement. Maybe you can identify with the women who cross their arms and tap their feet on the threshold, waiting for their husbands to prove themselves, or make a mess of things again. You grew up in the sixties and seventies with a strong sense of female dignity. You fought for your right to be heard and to penetrate the work force and the thinking world with your own perspective. And now it looks like someone might be taking that away from you.

The phrase "men's movement" means very different things to women. It's important that we acknowledge and include responses to this movement from women on all sides of the issue. And there are extremes.

In contrast to the banner waving overhead at the Detroit Silverdome, proclaiming "Men don't own women and children," the Oakland floating message was "Jesus loves you." That didn't mean there was no opposition.

On the contrary, a small group of picketers from the National Organization of Women took up residence in front of the stadium.

Perhaps they would have agreed with the disgruntled wife who wrote a letter in response to the July 31 *People* article on Promise Keepers entitled "Old Ways, New Men."

If what my husband wants is a happy wife and a happy marriage, then let him ask me what it takes. I do not need a group of male pigs to decide what I need. Our marriage was supposed to be a partnership between the two of us — private, equal and sacrosanct. Never, in any vows, did I agree to allow my marriage to be run by a group of any kind. My husband betrays me and our relationship by relegating me, my opinions, and my needs to the status of a child, while he proclaims himself and his cohorts to be always right, all-knowing, and infallible merely by being male. Somewhere there may be a wife who really does want her husband at those meetings, but this wife is suing for divorce and naming Promise Keepers as the cause.

I wonder about this woman's bitterness. Did her husband miss the point and apply leadership without serving?

I met a man in the Oakland airport who was going home to an empty house. "I was a take-charge kind of guy. I'd push my way around," he told me. His first time at Promise Keepers the previous year was "the straw that broke the camel's back. When I got home, she left me." He admitted that by then he had done enormous damage to her self-esteem.

In Search of the Big Picture

Do men come home from these "gatherings" and badger their wives into submission? Do they claim superiority and infallibility? Do they repress their wives' personalities and skills? It's possible. But it's not likely. No doubt some men are not hearing or applying the truth they've been given. But I've seen nothing in the movement that would encourage a man to abuse his leadership position.

Anytime questions are raised regarding roles, leadership, power, position in male/female relationships, someone gets hot flashes. Is there a way to encourage men, or women for that matter, to fit into a role without raising questions from those who don't understand?

Ken Canfield, in *Beside Every Great Dad*, points out that with the extremes of both the feminist movement and the present men's movement, "you actually see the inability of two movements to forgive each other. They both seek to be empowered by somehow stealing from the power base of the other, convinced that if one is strong, the other by necessity must be made weak. Christian men and women, however, can find *their* power from an outside source. And God's power is accessed by forgiving one another."[1]

The first observation we can make is that this sort of competition is not the thrust behind the men's movement. Its leaders will assure you it's not necessary for a man's leadership to usurp a woman's abilities. I love Canfield's phrase, "stealing from the power base." These guys will tell you they've discovered that outside source of power and that the battle is over.

Some women have voiced their concerns about the deep friendships their husbands are building with other men. I asked my "interview team" from chapter two that question:

"Tell me about these new relationships men are building with each other."

TIM: *It hurts some women to think their husbands can love another guy so much. But it's not that he doesn't love her. We're talking a different type of love, meeting a different need. One of the things I think wives can do is not be so jealous of these relationships that are out there.*

STEVE: *But if a woman is loved, she won't be jealous. So the key is to love your wife so that there's no insecurity there.*

TIM: *When we love them as Christ loved the church, they know we'd die for them.*

As I've questioned men about this issue, they're careful to make distinctions between the kind of love a man feels for his wife and the kind he feels for his friends. They assure me that the focus of these deep friendships is not to detract from intimacy with their wives, but to build a structure of accountability to help them follow through with promises and commitments they make. And it gives them the base of friendships women have long enjoyed.

Crossroads Ahead

It's Sunday afternoon, and you're perched in your favorite stuffed chair, wrapped up in the old stadium blanket you keep stashed behind it for just such an occasion. Your husband's away at a men's retreat. In your mind is this man of yours and questions about what this weekend will mean to you.

Let's hear more from our interview with leaders in the men's movement:

"What's the worst mistake a wife can make when her husband has just joined this men's movement?"

GARY: *Probably to say anything. When a man has encapsulated the soul of his heart with work, with pornography, with TV, with money, with toys — whatever — then he goes to PK, the Holy Spirit penetrates him. When he comes home, he is at his most teachable moment.*

The typical guy walks in pumped, and if he gets a negative response, it can set his heart back and push him down to the bottom. So when I suggest not to say anything, I mean to be prayerful, to be anticipatory, but to allow God to work in that guy's heart.

And certainly wives can say thank you. That's wonderful. But if the woman's woundedness comes out right at that point, it will crush his spirit.

RON: *That kind of confrontation will close his spirit. I think we're a lot more sensitive than women are, in that respect. Timing is critical.*

"There's a place for her feelings to come out, isn't there?"

GARY: *Absolutely. Just not at that moment.*

TIM: *When he's just gotten home, if she takes over, she's also drawing battle lines. She can usurp his position in his family and his marriage by a mere put-down. Here's God trying to work in his life. He's wanting to come home and be a leader and a lover, and then she says, "You'll never change. I don't care if you go off to some little pep rally and do some Jesus thing."*

She's basically saying, "I'm in the driver's seat because you weren't in it," or "I'm getting in it because I don't trust you," or "You're not going to get in it, so don't even tell me about what happened." But her reaction — if you think of it in terms of the parable of the seed — might come when what has just been planted by God hasn't had time to take root, and it can be easily snatched out.

"What's the best piece of advice you'd give a wife whose husband is going through a spiritual revival?"

GARY: *Follow him; join him; sense the protection that God has provided for him and for you.*

TIM: *The best thing she could do is make time for her prayer closet. Just continue to pray for that man and be a responder to what God is doing in his life, rather than a reactor. God can use that.*

God takes us a lot of different directions to get us where He wants us to be. There's not a definite left-right-left-right cadence to life. It's a dance, and you've got to figure out what the rhythm is in your marriage. The reason I could never be a woman is that I can't dance backwards. I

can't figure out how to know where his feet are going next. But a
woman who knows how to dance — it's amazing. She links arms with
him, he takes off, and she just moves in rhythm.

You might say that our marriages are at the crossroads. Maybe our husbands have been wandering along on a country road with no direction whatever. But now they've changed course, and here they come.

And, by the way, these guys are asking directions! They're reading the Map and coming to the place where their roads and destinations cross ours and God's. What's going to happen when we hit the intersection?

Here are some things we can and should do to help our husbands at the crossroads:

- Let your husband have time to process what he's learned by withholding your questions and evaluations until the future.
- Put your own needs aside for a short while so he'll have time and room to focus on his new goals.
- Let God have his way. We don't need to worry about the end result. When we do, it's easy to interfere.
- Encourage your husband's newfound friendships. There's room, time, and affection for both kinds of relationships. It's healthy for them and for us.
- Let your husband see the love and affection that allow him to change in front of you without embarrassment or harassment.
- Encourage your husband's growth by anticipating it, not challenging him to prove himself.
- Pray, pray, pray — for your husband and his growth, for your proper response, for the nation and what it needs from godly men.

Madeleine, Charlie's wife, finished our earlier conversation with a warning. "I'm dealing with friends now whose husbands have gone to Promise Keepers. These friends sit back with arms folded, scowls on their faces, waiting to see what happens. Actually, they're claiming failure and not giving

God a chance to work," she says. "It takes a strong man to say to his wife, 'You don't believe in me or in what God can do. But I'm going to honor God first by obeying him, and honor you as well by following through on what I've promised.'"

That kind of principled response is what's being preached in the men's movement and typically what's being carried out at home. But implementing promises makes for quite a bit of change in a household. What's your response going to be?

Promising Conversations

> Philippians 2:3–4 — *Do nothing from selfishness or empty conceit,*
> *but with humility of mind let each of you regard one another as more*
> *important than himself; do not merely look out for your own personal*
> *interests, but also for the interests of others.*

A woman's response to change in her husband is a product of all she is —
her background, her parenting, her self-image, her self-worth, her view of
God, and her maturity.

1. In your opinion, what is involved in a healthy response to positive
   change in another person?

2. How do you give your husband time to process what he's learned?

3. How do you put your needs aside?

4. How can you get out of God's way?

5. How can you practically love your husband so he can change without embarrassment?

Private Consideration

Read Matthew 25:14–30, the "Parable of the Talents." In the parable, the servants who made the most of their situations by investing the talents (money) received their master's blessing. The one who didn't invest not only missed the blessing but lost the talent as well. One application of this passage for wives is to capitalize on the opportunity God has put in our laps.

Specifically, what new opportunities (to grow, to change, to wait, to accept) do you see God handing you?

The fact is that life is either hard and satisfying
or easy and unsatisfying.

RICHARD LEIDER

CHAPTER FOUR

Change Has a Way

Stacy, my dentist's assistant, held my hand while the doctor injected Novocaine into my cheek. "I don't like change of any kind," she said. "It makes me uncomfortable. I don't even like changing the furniture around. My husband's the one who does that."

Unable to utter anything intelligible, I lifted my eyebrows and thought, "Moving furniture? I love it. It's like getting a whole new living room at no expense." Even so, I understood Stacy's aversion to change.

Some kinds of changes worry or challenge me, too. If change is imminent because of pressure or comes because of loss or disaster, I have a hard time sleeping. When my husband changes — the one I count on to stay the same, to be predictable — it's downright threatening. It means I have to change as well, in one way or another. It's not my choice anymore. It may even require me to move out of the way to accommodate his way of doing things.

Even when the change is good and necessary — sometimes I prefer the same old familiar bad habits!

Mary and David are parents to three-year-old twin girls and two older sons from his previous marriage. When God got hold of David, just two years ago, David made an about-face in the way he spent his time. After being a workaholic on the job and around the house, he transferred his energies to several ministries that take a great deal of time.

Mary's torn. She's thrilled by his new focus but frustrated by the time he gives it. Thrilled that he's hearing more about how to be a godly husband and father. Frustrated that he can't seem to practice what he hears. Thrilled by their twin girls. Frustrated that David doesn't sense her need for a break from them.

This is when change really hits home. The goals might be desirable, but the interim is a pain. No wonder change, and dealing with it, has recently been the subject of many books. It's a subject worth reviewing. Here are some basics to remember about the experience we call "change."

Change is taking place all the time. From the first moment we peek out at the world to the final moment when we leave it, our lives are moving. Physically, we grow up, out, and old. Mentally, we go from learning to spell our names to memorizing our bank "PIN" numbers. Emotionally, spiritually — in *every* area we change.

Psychology Today writer Nancy Schlossberg puts it this way: "Crisis, transition and change occur all through life. People are continually at the beginning, in the midst of and resolving transitions, some expected, some not."[1]

Change happens in two ways — controlled and uncontrolled. When we choose to cut our hair, switch jobs, or rearrange furniture, we are in control of the change. But when our children get sick or our husbands get serious with God, our control level falls down near zero. Understandably, we're a lot more comfortable if *we* orchestrate what happens, when, and how much. "The uncontrollable aspect of change is what drives us all a little wild," says New York psychotherapist JoAnn Magdoff. But she goes on to add, "The paradox is that we must be open to change in order to grow, but we still have to drag ourselves kicking and screaming through the upheaval."[2]

Change is biblical. Though God is unchangeable, He is in the business of change! His plan for us is filled with it. Remember Philippians 1:6? "Being confident of this, that he who began a good work in you will carry it on to completion until the day of Christ Jesus" (NIV). That's one of the reasons He allowed us to marry our husbands. As they grow, they stimulate further growth and change in our lives.

When you think about it, there's great comfort in knowing God can take us from one point in our lives to another. Change is part of His strategy, part of His work in our lives. He could have made us complete beings, born grown-up, already containing all we need for life. Instead, He wanted us to experience the motion of change, the adventure of both planned and unplanned adjustments.

Change takes time. Change tends to come like a child's growth. You don't notice the daily growth of your child. Then one morning you're staring at his nose instead of the top of his head. Even "overnight" change must be assimilated and adjusted to. It's a process. Whether you're moving from New York to New Jersey or adjusting from a never-home husband to one suddenly underfoot, transitions take time.

Men Are Not from Mars

Stan and Nancy both see the need for Stan's leadership of their home. "But Stan is like a steamroller," Nancy says. "The same day he started writing the checks, he wanted us to join a couple's Bible study. I can't handle it!"

Stan and Nancy's problem is not unique; men and women handle change differently. Warren Farrell, in *Why Men Are the Way They Are*, says, "When it comes to relationships, as opposed to business, men seldom change until they have to. But when they do, they often change quite quickly."

A man's goal is to get there, and fast, almost as if change is a competitive sport for them. They measure it: How long did it take me to get in the habit of listening to her with my full attention? Did I do it right? Did I do it better than someone else?

"Women on the other hand," says Farrell, "often relish the process of relationship change."[3] Our goal is to get there as well, but we pay more attention to the "getting" than the "there." This process spills over into our friendships. It's why we can sit around so long, talking with our friends about our problems, hopes, and dreams. Perhaps it partially explains why many more women than men watch talk shows and soap operas.

Understanding how each of us approaches change helps us see why our husbands are doing what they're doing and why we're reacting as we are. Obviously a smart approach to change makes use of the different ways husbands and wives handle it. The trick is working off each other's strengths.

Ready or Not

In addition to gender or personality differences, your present situation is a large factor in how you respond to change. Is the change perceived as good or bad? Is it *happening* in hard times or *bringing* hard times? Here are a few responses to change you might recognize:

"I'm ready!" Ann had pretty much raised the kids. Her husband, Matt, was a truck driver and usually made it home only on weekends or in the early morning hours. Sometimes when he was home, he'd try to handle the kids, but more often than not he undid the ground rules established by Ann during the week.

As the years went by, it seemed easier to live separate lives; Matt did his trucking, and Ann took care of the family. But when seniority gave Matt a local truck route, all the avoided, living-together issues came rushing back. "Divorce" found its way into more than one of their heated conversations.

After counseling and recommitment to Christ's will for their marriage, Matt starting asking Ann out on dates and looking for opportunities to get to know his wife. "We're talking, really talking these days," says Ann. "I feel like we're getting to know each other in ways we never have before." But what about him interfering with the house and her routine? "After twenty-five years of balancing checkbooks and worrying over the kids, I'm ready for a change. If he doesn't do it my way, I don't care. I'm tired of doing it alone."

For some women like Ann, the day-to-day struggles to change seem nothing compared to the overall heaviness of the past years. Their hearts are ready, willing, and eager for change, and the uncomfortableness of it is insignificant.

"Help! You're rocking the boat." I still have vivid memories of the morning we left our first house in eastern Pennsylvania for Ron's new job in Southern California. Matt was three years old. Molly had been born one month before. As the movers walked out of the house with the last of our furniture, I sat in a corner of the dining room, holding my new baby in my arms, and sobbed and sobbed. I can remember the sunlight and shadows, the bare white walls and the green carpet. I didn't want to leave. My children had been born in that city; my mentors were there.

I felt miserable. But the move was right, and Ron was excited.

Even when we understand the benefits of a transition, it can leave us feeling distressed. We haven't shut ourselves off from making the change — we just aren't welcoming it wholeheartedly. Change is rocking our boat, meddling with our security.

"I'm scared." Helen and Phil have three children, a nice home, and a comfortable lifestyle. He owns a survey company that provides a good income but demands a lot of his time. A couple of years ago Phil's relationship with God got much deeper. Men's retreats strengthened his commitment.

Recently he received an offer on his business. He's been talking it over with Helen. "Honey, remember our dream to open a Christian school? We both have our teaching degrees. Could this be God's way of directing us into a whole new ministry for our lives?"

Helen is scared, and she's asking her own questions. Could they keep up the house payments? Would she have to go back to pinching every nickel at the grocery store? What would such a big change do to the kids? What about college money?

God may not give us "a spirit of fear," but it's a real feeling that we can't just brush off. Until God works through it with us, our hearts aren't free to make the change — even if our bodies must.

"I'll believe it when I see it." Linda's husband, Darrell, is a pastor. He's also a jealous man. Linda's outgoing personality and position as a pastor's wife often bring her into brief contact with men in the church. She's careful in her behavior and faithful to Darrell. Yet over and over he's accused her of flirting or inviting the advances of men in the congregation.

In hurt and confusion, Linda's tried everything from high-collared clothes to virtual seclusion. Nothing's worked, and for years she's lived with false accusations, hurtful words, and until-the-next-time apologies.

Darrell loves God, but it wasn't until he started meeting with other men that he realized he had a problem. In remorse he confessed his jealousy to God and then went to Linda. But his confession felt like another empty apology. She'll believe his change when she sees it.

Women like Linda have lost hope of change. In order to function, they've closed down a part of their hearts.

Whether your heart is wide open to your husband's change or mostly cut off to it, the self-check test at the end of this chapter might help you learn something about how you handle change. If you're struggling with a negative response, there's hope, and there's a way to make it better.

The Art of Change

In business, the companies that are innovative lead the market. In fashion, new styles get the media coverage and the mark-up. Even in our daily lives we look for more expedient ways to get our work done, more efficient ways to organize our closets, more creative ways to use our time.

We can also be creative and innovative about how we handle change in our marriage. Here are some ideas:

Accept the stages. A first step is to understand that basically change has four stages to it, whether we're the "changers" or the "changees."

- First, we recognize the need for change.
- Second, we accept our responsibility to change or to allow change. We own it.
- Third, we start working at it (i.e., we begin a new habit, or we allow someone to begin one).
- Fourth, the change is now part of a lifestyle.

Let's apply these steps to several familiar scenarios.

Diaper changing: 1. We recognize the need. 2. We accept our responsibility to change that diaper. 3. We learn how to do it and begin doing it. 4. We do it as often as necessary.

Good eating habits: 1. We recognize the need. 2. We accept our responsibility to eat right. 3. We read, learn to shop well, and cook differently. 4. Good eating habits become a lifestyle.

Fathering: 1. Your husband recognizes the need to be a better father. You recognize that God wants him in that role. 2. He accepts the responsibility to grow in that area. You accept the responsibility to let him try and, if necessary, fail. 3. He studies and reads and decides he should put the kids to bed at night and pray with them. You let him, and assist him if he asks you for help. 4. He becomes more and more confident as a father. You become more and more confident in his fathering. Now you have him to shoulder more of the responsibility.

Once you recognize the stages of change, you'll be better able to adapt to, and be patient with, the sometimes lengthy process. Instead of looking at your husband and saying, "Nothing's happening!" you can say, "Yes, he is at that point, and that's encouraging." The trick is not to attach your own timetable to the stages.

Attempt one thing at a time. Some of our guys have had a really powerful wake-up call. God has taken hold of them and flashed their lives before their eyes. Everywhere they look they're confronted with grave inadequacies. When they come home after they've come face to face with themselves, they probably expect us to see all those weak spots, too. And most likely we do.

Being more sensitive and romantic, improving as a father, taking leadership, committing more fully to Christ — we're talking changes that can affect everything from work schedules to dinner-table routines. Trying to get our husbands to tackle them all at once is like putting a bomb under our own bed. Only a rare man, if any, could handle a major overhaul all at once. And only a rare woman, if any, could handle being in the same house with a man attempting a major overhaul.

When we're making major changes in our lives and looking for them to last, taking on too much is like wrapping our lips around the proverbial fire hose. We can't take it. Our husbands can't take it. Our marriages can't take it. We need to love enough to wait it out and take it slow.

Apply the twenty-one-day rule — with mercy. Authorities say it takes twenty-one consecutive days (or twenty-one consecutive tries) to convert an action into a habit. What that says to me is that time is a factor. It takes time to adjust to new ways of doing things.

Suppose your husband is working to be that better father we mentioned earlier. And in his attempts to establish healthy bedtime rituals and significant "father-bonding," he declares pillow fights mandatory every night. My first inclination would be to shout, "Are you crazy? Getting them all wound up when they should be winding down?" But his efforts to be a better dad need rewarding. Letting him live through the consequences for several nights, when Bobby is still awake for the eleven o'clock news, is probably all the lesson he needs.

I can almost guarantee that it won't take twenty-one nights of the late news with Bobby for a growing dad to make some adjustments. But it might take longer than that to get the good routine, the good habits, established. It's worth the wait.

Acknowledge your assets and make use of them. When Mary was stressed out over David's involvement in church and lack of help with the twins, she called me. Looking back, I realize I did little more than listen and assure her things were normal — but it helped.

Spiritually growing Christian friends and family members are an asset when our husbands' changes begin to frustrate, anger, or hurt us. They provide a place for us to "hear" our feelings. Sometimes that's all you need to put things into perspective.

Emotional Messages

While our husbands are changing, it's easy to sit back with that I'll-believe-it-when-I-see-it look on our faces. And many wives have plenty of experience to back up their skepticism. But nothing is more debilitating to growth than to have someone suspect it from the outset. That's why the emotional signals we send our men are so important. Often we don't realize what impact we're making — good and bad.

When you know someone is making an effort to change, pointing out failure is defeating. When Ron's on a diet, I need to encourage him by commenting on how well he's eating, not remind him of the junk food that occasionally slips past his lips.

Giselle, whose husband struggles to be the leader in his family, says, "Sometimes John reassures me that things will be different, but he lives it out for only two or three days. And yet each time there's a change I believe it's genuine. I grant him a 100 percent clean slate. I have to do that to model Christ. And it's what I would want if I were the one trying to grow."

Sometimes progress is just plain invisible. In those cases it's easy for our husbands to get discouraged and for us to miss a lot. Vicki and Frank, according to Warren Farrell, are working on a small change:

"You agreed to put the toilet seat down, and you still always leave it up," Vicki complained.

"I almost always put it down," Frank retorted.

In fact, Vicki could recall half a dozen times she had almost fallen into the toilet in the past month alone. And Frank could recall at least two dozen times he had put it down. Change is like that. The person changing is aware of each time the toilet seat is put down. The person living with her or him notices only when the toilet seat is up.[4]

Change is like that. The person growing is very aware of doing the right thing; when he/she slips, it's an unintentional mistake. The person watching for growth is much more aware of the infractions than the positive change. Our nagging fears about whether this is real and will last tend to cause us to hunt for negatives.

It's natural to attempt to change behavior with disapproval, criticizing the wrong behavior to bring out the right. Unfortunately, that doesn't work. Criticism backfires. It's hunting for and praising the positives that make a positive emotional difference. Approval has always been a more effective way to encourage change.

When I talked with Mary, the wife of the workaholic husband, I could tell that her feelings were tying her up in bows. She'd praise David in one sentence, and in the next her need for help and recognition would come spilling out.

As we talked, I assured her that what she was feeling was common for mothers of young children. But I wanted her to put her feelings about David into perspective, so I asked her to make a list of all the ways David was changing and what she saw that she liked.

She thought about that. I could hear the difference in her tone of voice when she changed her perspective. David was a new Christian, just discovering what it all meant. She needed to keep in mind his starting point. She needed to give him emotional time and room to change. When Mary took the time to record David's growth on paper, it shifted her focus off herself and onto him.

If your husband is going through significant spiritual change in his life, your attitude toward change, your response to change, and your willingness to encourage him will make a huge impact. You're not always going to handle things the best way possible, but your heart will show through to the man who lives with you day after day. Will you rush ahead in overeager anticipation or come alongside and help?

Once you've answered that question, here's another one: What does your ideal changed man look like?

Self Test: How Do I Face Change?

1. "Honey, let's go to the coast (mountains, city, anywhere). Forget the yard and laundry; let's just go." Your response?

   A. You bet. Give me five minutes.

   B. But we need to...

   C. Can't you ever plan anything? Why do we always go on the spur of the moment?

   D. I need to wash some white clothes and get someone to take my Sunday School class — then I'd love to go.

2. "Honey, I think Jimmy is old enough to go fishing. I'll take him tomorrow." (Jimmy's five.) Your response?

   A. What a great idea.

   B. I don't think so.

   C. Honey, you don't watch Jimmy that well. What if he drowns?

   D. He has a PeeWee baseball game. We'd better see what he wants to do.

3. It's eight o'clock Saturday evening and the Christian Education director calls. "Rosanne's sick. Could you take her class tomorrow?" Your response?

A. Sure. No problem.

B. No way. I'm not prepared.

C. Hesitant. I know I should help, but I don't really want to.

D. Hesitant. It's a busy weekend. Should I try to fit one more thing in?

4. "Honey, I know you walk with Janie every day, but I can get home early on Tuesdays and Thursdays. Will you walk with me?" Your response?

A. I'd love that. I'll talk to Janie today.

B. This is my time with Janie.

C. I'm used to walking fast, and you're not really in shape. Why don't you start off with Bill?

D. It might work. Let me call Janie first and see if that works for her.

5. "Honey, come look at the new car I bought." Your response?

A. It's beautiful. I want to drive it.

B. You bought what?

C. We can't afford that. What are the monthly payments?

D. I wish you would have discussed it with me first.

6. Your husband has finally turned off the TV and is reading books that will help him be a better husband and father. Now two or three nights a week he works on his growth. Your response?

A. What a great answer to prayer!

B. Now he's spending more time reading than with me.

C. Couldn't you read in the other room so I can watch TV?

D. Is there anything I should be reading so we can grow together?

Insights:

If you marked mostly "A," change is easy for you.

If you marked mostly "B," change is difficult for you.

If you marked mostly "C," change brings out the negative side in you.

If you marked mostly "D," change is hard, but you try to work with it.

Promising Conversations

2 Corinthians 3:18 — *"But we all, with unveiled face beholding as in a mirror the glory of the Lord, are being transformed into the same image from glory to glory...."*

1. Take the verse above and construct a paraphrase that applies to your life.

2. How does change motivate or incapacitate you?

3. How do you react to changes in...

   furniture?

   weather, seasons?

   schedule?

   moods?

   location?

   career?

   relationships?

4. Can you think of any idioms, proverbs, phrases, encouraging sayings, or Bible verses that help you keep perspective in the middle of change? (For example, "A rolling stone gathers no moss." "For I, the Lord, do not change;" Malachi 3:6a.)

5. What's the best/worst example in the Bible of a wife's response to her husband's change?

Private Consideration

1 Corinthians 13:11 — *"When I was a child, I talked like a child, I thought like a child, I reasoned like a child. When I became a man, I put childish ways behind me"* (NIV).

Find a mirror and look at yourself, long and hard. Notice your wrinkles and any gray hair. Do you feel younger than you look? Most of us do. Looking at your relationships and responses to life, how fully have you made the transition from childishness to maturity?

Men do not become more lovable until they feel understood.

WARREN FARRELL, PH.D.

The Same Old Guy

I can pinpoint the moment I realized Ron was the man I loved and wanted to marry. I was in my parents' home in Denver, in the kitchen, and Ron was washing the dishes. (That's when my mom fell in love with him, too.) We'd been out in the sun, and it was a hot summer afternoon. Ron had taken off his shirt, and as he stood there at the sink I noticed again the blemishes on his back — and realized that I didn't care.

A skin problem had been enough to terminate any dating relationship in the past. (I wasn't a very deep young woman.) But I'd finally found a man whose inside was more important to me than his outside.

When we fall in love, our husbands-to-be are about as perfect as is humanly possible. Even their imperfections fit into our lovely picture of the future. But, as you well know, something often happens after the walk down the aisle — we unintentionally raise the standards for perfection, blemishes appear, and our new husbands just don't measure up.

If your husband has recently returned from some terrific men's retreat, or heard a great sermon on being a good husband, or come from the football stadium and a Promise Keepers' event, you're surely forming some wonderful pictures of the changes that are about to take place.

And the man snoring in front of the TV may be working hard on the same image. But what if you're not seeing the changes you want to see? What if he's the same old guy?

One husband, let's call him Kevin, came home excited about his new growth in the Lord. He'd attended a Man's Authentic Nature (MAN) conference in Colorado. His resulting enthusiasm all but took his wife's breath away.

Susan had been hoping for specific changes in Kevin's growth. What she'd wanted was a renewed commitment to help around the house and with their new baby. But what she got was even less notice of the household since Kevin used every spare moment for Bible study.

Susan feels guilty for resenting his new priorities. She knows Kevin's spiritual growth is essential; she just wants that spirituality to spill over to the dishes. Instead, she basically ended up with the same old guy.

Susan's not the only disillusioned wife.

We all have expectations of what a spiritual husband would look like. For most of us, our expectations unconsciously become spiritual ideals that we measure our men against. But is this fair?

Fantasy life — and fantasy men — have intrigued us from our first storybooks. When we were four, Cinderella and her prince captivated us. Then we got a bit more sophisticated and started a collection of Kens and Barbies. Take that perfect couple, add flesh and blood, hold the cellulite, pimples, and balding — and it's Tom Cruise and Nicole Kidman on the big screen — a fairy tale for grownups.

Even in our spiritual life, high-profile, godly men can stir our fantasies — Billy Graham, Chuck Swindoll, James Dobson. If only...

It's easy to enter our men in a comparison game they can't win. Even if their competition isn't Billy Graham, our own picture of the perfect godly man can become a sort of "spiritual pin-up." As a husband might compare his wife to some gorgeous, long-legged, younger model — and she despairs because she can't meet the standard — we can do the same with our men on a spiritual level.

Unveiling Your Spiritual Pin-Up

Think for a moment about your spiritual fantasy man. What's he like? Where did he come from? Our fantasies are born in our dreams, hopes, and experiences. Sometimes they're compilations of people we know; sometimes they look like our fathers, our pastors, our counselors, or our friends.

I can trace some of my ideals about men back to my father. It's taken me years to get over the fact that Ron is not more like my father in certain areas. Some of my dearest memories of my dad reflect his concern for the welfare of his three girls — or, admittedly, his overprotection.

On cold Denver mornings he'd heat up the car for thirty minutes before the drive to school. He constantly reminded "his girls" to keep the doors locked when we drove alone. He'd drive us anywhere, if it meant keeping us from having to ride the bus. He'd wait up if we were out late, and after my sisters moved out, he'd follow them home at night to their apartments, just to be sure they made it safely. He'd go out of his way to keep us from going out of our way.

The ideals I gathered from my dad's loving concern took a real knock right after Ron and I were married. One night Ron let me go out on an errand in the dark — alone! I couldn't believe it. And no admonition to keep my doors locked. My dad's ways were not Ron's. To this day if I want something at night, I get it. He even goes to sleep before I get home.

David Fogelson, an assistant clinical professor at UCLA Medical School, helps explain why fathers often influence our idealized spiritual pin-ups. "When your first major experience with an adult male is with your father, you tend to reproduce the quality of that relationship with men later in life — or to react against it."[1]

Even as our experiences with our fathers affect our expectations, so do a dozen other experiences with dates, friends, the media, churches. Once our ideal is formed, we wonder what it would be like to share our lives with such a godly man. We wonder, and we wish. But then we face reality across the dinner table.

Unknowingly we allow two men to lay claim to our hearts — a real one and an ideal one. In Matthew 6:24, Jesus makes it clear that our hearts cannot have a double allegiance. We'll love one, while despising the other. We need to identify and get rid of our fantasy before we can fully love our real guy.

The Measure of a Man

In a couple of informal surveys I asked several women what a spiritual man looks like. They said he...

- spends quality time in the Bible (that I can verify).
- spends quality time with the children (that I can prescribe).
- spends quality time with me (that meets my needs).
- initiates all of the above (without my saying anything).

My man is spiritual when...

- he reads instead of watching TV.
- he helps put the children to bed.
- he's a good provider.
- he prays with me.

What does your own measuring stick look like? The first several points that spring to my mind are definitely spiritual-sounding. But then I get down to the real nitty-gritty: Does he help with the dishes when I need him to? Does he leave the toilet seat up? Does he hog the remote control? Does he leave his clothes all over the bedroom floor?

Evelyn's husband, Bill, went to a Promise Keepers' rally in Boulder, Colorado. She'd heard great things from other wives about their husbands coming home more interested in their families. Her sister's husband even became a Christian at a rally, and their lives changed radically. Her one hope was that Bill would come home with some communication skills. She just wanted him to talk to her. Was that too much to ask?

Obviously spiritual growth should impact our husbands' behavior. Even the Scriptures state, "By their fruit you will recognize them" (Matthew 7:16a, NIV). But does that necessarily imply an invitation to take measurements? Does it give us the right as wives to hold up the biblical yardstick?

When Bill left for the rally, several of the women from Evelyn's church got together at a restaurant to compare expectations. A friend named Carol shared the booth with Evelyn and listened to her hope-filled description of "Bill, the Fantasy Husband Who Talks."

Carol could relate. She'd placed expectations on her husband the year before, but they weren't met the way she'd hoped. As she and God dealt with her disappointment, she came to realize how tiny her measuring stick was compared to God's. He measured the whole man from the inside, while she concentrated on a few of her own ideals from the outside.

Looking at Evelyn over their coffee, Carol said, "More than anything our husbands want to be loved for who they are. If they're changing, sometimes it's in spite of us. Forgive Bill for not being what *you* want him to be. Then let God make him into what *He* wants him to be."

About That Yardstick...

How do we stop measuring our husbands and start tearing down our "spiritual pin-ups"? It's not easy, especially when we see our men turning to God as never before and making promises to be better husbands and fathers. Unconsciously we keep checking to see if it's real and if it will last. Yet our scrutiny does nothing to make it real or make it last. If anything, it discourages us and our husbands. So when you're tempted to pull out the yardstick or draw a comparison, remember these four things:

1. *Your husband wishes he could measure up.* Our husbands, regardless of how much they might change, will never be perfect, and this knowledge can sting them. Robert Hicks writes in *Uneasy Manhood,* "One man told me, 'Between my boss, my wife, and my kids, at least one of them is mad at me every day for not being at something.'"[2]

That sentence makes my heart hurt. I so much want to release Ron from the pressure to be perfect, to fulfill my fantasies.

Ron's prayers have often frustrated me. He's been a Christian for thirty-four years, and he's been praying that long as well. Yet when we pray together, he still can get everything said in about seven minutes, tops. In seven minutes I've barely started.

For years I've interpreted Ron's short prayers as "Praying together is not that important."

Hicks explained this simply wasn't true. "Usually, the wife compares her husband's prayers (when he does pray with her) to what she thinks the standard of appropriate prayers should be — the pastor's [or hers, I might add].... I suggest that men pray the way they talk and women pray the way they talk.... Men should never feel inferior because they pray differently from their wives. The essential point is that they pray."[3]

2. *His growth is an invisible process.* When my daughter was born, no one looked at her and said, "What's wrong with your baby? She didn't grow half an inch yesterday." They didn't expect instant physical growth. They knew it takes time to add inches and pounds.

Yet when it comes to spiritual growth, we often adopt a microwave approach. If we don't see changes instantly, we think something is wrong. We forget that before outward behavior makes a lasting, substantial turn, a lot must take place on the inside.

My friend Julie knows this but still struggles to bite her tongue as she watches her immature son and recently saved daughter-in-law struggle in their new marriage. It's so tempting to interfere with the growth-by-experience and natural consequences her daughter-in-law must go through. What helps keep her quiet is remembering past experience. Years before, her brother and his wife, now sensitive and mature Christians, were in much the same place. "God's timing is so important," she said. "We look for the 'final' right now and forget the time it takes to get there."

Watching for growth is like watching a tooth grow, or the hour hand on a clock move. It's usually so slow we don't know it's happened until after the fact. It's like that moment when you realize your fifteen-year-old is a woman or your hair is much grayer than the last time you looked in the mirror.

Because growth is a process, measuring it is almost a violation. It says to the "grow-ee," "Hurry up! I'm watching and measuring, and I can't see it happening." Just as constant comments and comparisons about our children's physical growth can make them feel too small, too big, too short, or too tall, we can discourage a person who is growing spiritually. Our hovering presence can overwhelm the one we love.

3. *You can't measure what you don't know.* I know when my heart is soft. I know when my prayers are honest. I know when my mind wanders. I know when I read Scripture and really hear it, and when I read verse after verse while thinking about my day. I even have some pretty good ideas about my motives — when I act out of love or simply to impress someone. But I don't know these things about anyone else, including Ron. And I'm not alone.

Theresa met Mark when he came to work for her father. They married young, moved across the country, and had three daughters — all in a hectic three years. Life was chaotic but good. Then their son, Todd, was born. He was a spina bifida baby and brought with him a host of heart-crushing possibilities. The emotional and financial stress began wrapping around the couple like a boa constrictor.

Theresa went into depression right after Todd was born, grieving over her son's condition — and hurt and confused that Mark didn't seem to be grieving at all. He was never there. He left early in the morning and stayed out late into the evening, often missing dinner. She never saw him cry.

The weight of Todd's condition, combined with three little girls and an absent husband and father, built up inside Theresa until she exploded one night when Mark walked in the door. "Todd is four months old! He is alive! You never hold him. I just need to know that you love him!"

Mark felt crushed to be accused so bitterly and so openly. His daughters stared saucer-eyed at their mother. As Theresa disappeared into the living room to cry alone, Mark quietly and quickly straightened up the kitchen and put his daughters to bed. Then, like all the other nights since Todd's birth, he knelt by Todd's crib, buried his head in his hands, and sobbed. He prayed softly but fervently for his son and for his family, asking God for peace to invade his household.

That night, for the first time, Theresa saw Mark on the floor of Todd's room. His shoulders shook with emotion as he prayed and cried. That sight released her tension. She went to Mark, and they spent the next several hours in each other's arms, praying over Todd, talking through the previous four months, and sharing hopes for the future.

Theresa finally realized she was requiring Mark to grieve in front of her, to respond to this difficult slice of life in a way she could see, measure, and understand. But he couldn't — and it wasn't necessary. She asked Mark's forgiveness for judging what she didn't know.

4. *Your husband expresses his spirituality differently than you.* Like so much of what we are and do, our spirituality is wrapped up in our personalities, our backgrounds, and our particular circumstances. For some men, being spiritual means reading Bible stories to their preschoolers. For others it's tied to Bible translations and worship styles. For some women, it means dressing up on Sunday. For others, it's taking time to attend a weekly Bible study.

Which is right? What's spiritual?

I read my Bible with a pen in hand. I have friends who wouldn't ever consider writing in their Bibles. My husband can pray deeply at McDonalds. I can't handle distractions and need a quiet place. Others pray when they walk, and some pray on their knees. Is one better or more spiritual than another?

By God's design, everyone's faith is expressed uniquely. Look at the variety in the disciples that Jesus chose. He had quiet followers like Nathaniel, loud ones like Peter, adoring ones like John, and detailed ones like Mark. Yet so often we make no allowances for each person's unique spirituality. We measure others by what brings us close to God. This is especially true when it comes to our husbands.

"Men have their own unique spirituality," Robert Hicks says. "If their brains work differently, their tongues speak differently, they work and experience their relationships differently, their spiritual approach will also be unique. Their masculine uniqueness will color their tastes and needs in the realm of spiritual pursuits as well.... There is a critical need to understand and make allowances for the male perspective and appreciate his unique contributions and approaches to the Christian life."[4]

For years Debbie thought Art wasn't growing in his faith. She couldn't understand his lack of willingness to talk and pray with her. But then he was diagnosed with terminal cancer.

"I so misjudged him," Debbie says. "During those quiet years he was growing in ways I couldn't see. But I saw it when he told our children of his illness, when he went back and forth to the hospital, and when he held my hand and told me that all the good we shared would be gold, silver, and precious jewels."

Love Beyond Measure

God's primary goal in being a part of our lives, and our husbands' lives, is to create and maintain a love relationship with us. He wants us to get to know

Him better. He orchestrates everything in our lives to make that happen, including pairing us up with another fallible, imperfect human being. He knows you and me and what our characters need for refining. He knows our men, their good and bad parts, and what they'll be when they grow up. And before our eyes He's stirring the pot and heating up the fire so that the end result will be that we know Him better.

If we continue to pressure our "same old guys," refusing to accept the men God made and the men He's making, we will miss God's blessing and push away His hand. That scares me. It also scares me to think I might choose a fantasy world, apart from God, avoiding the work and the pain that are necessary for growing.

As Elisabeth Elliott says in her book *Let Me Be a Woman*, "Marriage is a choice of one above all others.... Any choice we ever make in life instantly limits us. To choose to take this man as your husband is to choose not to take every other man on earth. When you decide to marry this particular sinner, you have committed yourself to putting up with his particular sins even though you don't have a very clear idea of what they will be."[5]

We didn't marry our husbands by accident. Or maybe we did! But now our marriage is a reality, and God has His plan, regardless of what put us together in the first place. If we've been holding out for perfection, it's time we forgave our men for not being spiritual giants that meet our needs. It's time to slacken the rope, release the pressure, and accept our husbands for who they are and who God is making them to be.

Our real men have love handles and pot bellies, they scratch and burp and drop their underwear on the floor. They watch TV when they should be reading good books, and take our children to see *Terminator* instead of *Little Women*. They're still the same old guys, trying to change some of the same old things.

Lord, may we love them *beyond* measure.

Promising Conversations

1 Corinthians 13:4–8a — *"Love is patient, love is kind, and is not
jealous; love does not brag and is not arrogant, does not act unbecom-
ingly; it does not seek its own, is not provoked, does not take into
account a wrong suffered, does not rejoice in unrighteousness, but
rejoices with the truth; bears all things, believes all things, hopes all
things, endures all things. Love never fails...."*

1. This passage can often be overlooked because it is so familiar. But it
   reminds us that love is an action, something we do. How do you
   measure up, on a scale of one to five, with one being pathetic and five
   being terrific?

love is patient	1	2	3	4	5
love is kind	1	2	3	4	5
love is not jealous	1	2	3	4	5
love does not brag	1	2	3	4	5
love isn't arrogant	1	2	3	4	5
love doesn't act unbecomingly	1	2	3	4	5
love doesn't seek its own	1	2	3	4	5
love is not provoked	1	2	3	4	5
love doesn't take into account a wrong suffered	1	2	3	4	5
love doesn't rejoice in unrighteousness	1	2	3	4	5
love rejoices in the truth	1	2	3	4	5
love bears all things	1	2	3	4	5
love believes all things	1	2	3	4	5
love hopes all things	1	2	3	4	5
love endures all things	1	2	3	4	5
love never fails	1	2	3	4	5

2. What kinds of unexpected changes are your husband's changes requiring of you?

Private Consideration

Proverbs 13:12 — *"Hope deferred makes the heart sick, but desire fulfilled is a tree of life."*

Isaiah 40:31 — *"Yet those who wait for the LORD will gain new strength; they will mount up with wings like eagles, they will run and not get tired, they will walk and not become weary."*

Allow yourself to think objectively about your husband. Look at what you consider his strengths and weaknesses. Think about them in light of what could be true of him.

1. What's changing in your husband's life? How is he staying the same?

2. What had you hoped to see?

A man's home is not his castle so much as his monastery, and if he happens to be treated like a king there, then it is only so that he might be better enabled to become a servant.... For there is no way to surrender the will except by surrendering it to another will.

MIKE MASON

Who's Leading Whom?

Once upon a time, there was a beautiful queen who ruled over an idyllic queendom. Her king used to wear the lance in the family, but he abdicated his throne to his wife when he realized what a gem she was. (In other words, he married well, but I'm not so sure she did.)

Things were running smoothly. Really they were. But an undercurrent of discontent ran among the families in the queendom. You see, following the king's example, many of the men in the community set aside their responsibilities as husbands and fathers. They let their wives run the ramparts. The children, bereft of virtuous fathers, lacked discipline and dreamt of welfare, not work.

One day while the king was lying under a tree watching his queen joust with a neighboring ruler, the Truth came upon him. Deep inside this discontented man was a true king, a leader struggling to get out. He thought back to a Book he'd read as a child about the lives of several kings. The weak kings, the ones who lost all the battles and whose children were disappointing, looked a lot like him. The strong kings, who with their families made a mark on the people and changed history, looked quite different.

What if, in giving over his responsibilities to his queen, he was giving away something that Truth had given him? A crown, a position that gave him strength, structure, and a design for his life. Slowly it dawned on him: When he gave the crown away, he had no one to be and nothing to do.

That night, before a feast of wild game, greens, and mineral water, the king proclaimed himself king again.

His queen was now facing a dilemma. Should she or shouldn't she? Her choice was obvious — turn the queendom back into a kingdom, or keep the power herself.

What do you think the queen did? Perhaps your answer is indicative of what you might do in a similar situation. It just depends, doesn't it? Was the queen as disillusioned as the king in the end? What would she lose if she let the king take over again? Would he be as good a leader as she? Or would he do things differently?

You may find yourself asking similar questions these days about your husband. Within the current Christian men's movement, thousands of husbands arrived at their gatherings, feeling like court jesters, and have come home encouraged to resume leadership of their families. Certainly they're not encouraged to *act* like kings or dictators, but they are asked to take ultimate responsibility for their families' welfare.

Maybe that's just what you've been waiting for. Or maybe not. The issue of male leadership is almost always a sticky one, partly because it leaves so much room for misinterpretation and partly because it naturally feels threatening and confusing to women who have experienced its abuse.

Before we can objectively and honestly answer the question of whether and how a wife should hand over the kingdom, let's look at the way this question has played out in the history of the church.

The History of His Reign

Until recently, the evangelical church taught that if a husband determined it, a wife obeyed it, and that settled it. For a Christian woman to question her husband's decisions, much less overturn them, was always wrong. Obedience to a husband's leadership was a woman's definition of being a godly wife.

Many men, operating under this concept of leadership, formed dictatorships. Benevolent husbands tried to rule in love; less-than-perfect ones left their wives with the family responsibilities they didn't want but kept the power; others abused the power and their wives. These men traded their husband/father roles for control, ignoring the scriptural admonitions to protect their wives from violence, insignificance, inequality, and other mistreatment.

Women under this kind of authority often raised the kids and ran the home while having little say in money matters, little time to develop talents, and little power in making decisions.

Bill and Ginny, married eight years, are a modern-day example of this kind of leadership. When Ginny suffered a major illness, Bill became a Christian, and Ginny recommitted her life to Christ. From the start, Bill was a strong guy with definite views on submission.

One time when Bill was gone for the day on business, Ginny, his unpaid executive secretary, needed a rather large sum of money to help pay an emergency bill. She didn't have enough in their checking account to cover the bill, so she dipped into their savings account, fully intending to report the transfer to Bill as soon as she saw him. She wanted to tell him face to face and explain her need, so she passed up an opportunity to tell him on the phone.

When he got back, and before she had the opportunity to explain, he discovered the shortage and accused her of stealing from the company. The idea that she had spent money without his approval gravely upset him. The idea that he'd shoot first and ask questions later upset her. The incident deeply rattled their marriage.

Leadership: Long Debated, Still Awaited

In opposition to the flaws of a "dictatorship," many couples have found an alternative. They've traded the concept of leadership for that of equal partnership. *No one* needs to lead. Proponents of this philosophy naturally oppose the men's movement's encouraging male leadership at home.

Christine Martin from New York City put it more than bluntly when she wrote a letter to *People* magazine (August 21, 1995): "The male chauvinism of the Promise Keepers is sickening and moronic. Husband and wife should be equal partners. If one is to have more say in a decision than the other, common sense would mandate that it be whoever has more intelligence or insight regarding the issue to be decided."

Put in different terms, an equal partnership sounds a lot less threatening than a one-party, husband leadership — especially in light of past abuse. As a result many Christian families today order their homes with the equal partnership approach. But the equal idealism isn't always panning out.

Michael Lamb, Ph.D., chief of the section on social and emotional development at the National Institute of Child Health and Human Development in Bethesda, Maryland, says, "Fathers are doing more than they were, but they are still functioning primarily as people who 'help out.' We still have not seen a significant shift in the perception of just who holds the responsibility for the family."[1]

What's more, according to General Social Surveys done by the Opinion Research Center at the University of Chicago from the 1970s to the 1990s, the happiness of married people has dramatically decreased, especially for women. Speculation about the unhappiness of married women supports the observation that "Since most women now stay in the labor force after marriage, the biggest change in their lives after marriage may be an increase in responsibilities."[2]

Even in the homes where responsibilities are more evenly shared, problems arise when agreements can't be reached. Mike and Jeanne were married seventeen years and had three children. They were active in church and Bible studies but struggled over handling the kids and finances. Each strongly believed that neither one had the right to lead the other. Each also believed that he or she had the correct approach to handling money and the children. For years this couple went round and round, often making decisions independently. Finally in total frustration they separated. More than once, at the urging of their Christian friends, they tried to reconcile. But when one was willing to try, the other said, "Only under these conditions." Of course, setting conditions meant one was still trying to lead or control the other. Eventually they divorced.

No wonder more and more men are looking for answers to the tender questions of leadership. Is there really *an* answer — one right way? Yes, and no.

Leadership, Bible-Style

The answer to our questions about leadership lies within the pages of our Bibles. Accepting what others teach should only come after a personal, "ask the Holy Spirit for help" search for ourselves. As our husbands blow the dust off their Bibles and dig into the issue of home leadership, here is what they're finding.

Verses like Ephesians 5:23, 1 Corinthians 11:3, and 1 Timothy 3:4 make it clear that God intends men to take leadership in the home. But what does that leadership look like?

The world's definition of leadership, which associates it with power, is not the same as the Bible's. Biblical leadership, demonstrated by the leaders God provided for people and families, involves meeting the real and felt needs of a person or group of people.

A leader is a need-meeter, a servant.

This servant-leader is described in Thessalonians by Paul (an aggressive,

Type A apostle), Silvanus (the administrative type), and Timothy (the youngest of the three, who was timid in his leadership). Three different types of leaders worked together for the same purpose, modeling the same qualities.

In 1 Thessalonians 2:7–12, these leaders flesh out the simple definition that "biblical leadership is meeting the real and felt needs of a person." They describe qualities that apply to both men and women. Good leaders of either gender need all ten of these qualities. Leaders are to...

1. be a team (note the frequency of the word "we")

2. be consistent (2:7 — "we proved to be")

3. be gentle as a nursing mother (2:7)

4. be affectionate (2:8 — "having thus a fond affection...you had become very dear to us")

5. effectively communicate the truth (2:8–9 — the gospel)

6. be transparent (2:8 — "but also our own lives")

7. work hard (2:9 — "working night and day")

8. have a serving spirit (2:9 — "so as not to be a burden")

9. have a holy lifestyle (2:10 — "how devoutly and uprightly and blamelessly we behaved toward you believers")

10. exhort, encourage and implore like a father (2:11 — "as a father would his own children")

And all this so that those who follow "may walk in a manner worthy of the God who calls you into His own kingdom and glory" (2:12).

Note that these ten qualities are neither gender specific nor personality specific. They're the qualities that make a man good at leading his family. And they're the qualities that make a woman a good leader as well. They're also the qualities that make mothers and fathers good parents.

What about the fact that the Bible says wives are to be submissive and a helpmate? The Greek word for submission is *hupotasso*, which means "to place oneself under a leader to ensure victory in battle." The actual biblical word for submission has nothing to do with weakness, subservience, or passivity. In the Bible the word is used in such a way that makes it our choice, not our husband's.

Our call to be submissive (Ephesians 5:22; Colossians 3:18; 1 Peter 3:1) is an action we take, not one our husbands make us take. It is our choosing to join our independence to that of another independent being so we can both work better.

Submission is our decision to serve another person. It is not the same as *submersion*. God has designed the husband and wife to be interdependent but not independent. Those two words are related but are so different. As men and women we are to be fully functioning adults, with our own personalities, our own abilities, temperaments, strengths, weaknesses. But in a marriage we are not to be so fully functioning that we don't need the other.

I like to think we're similar to chopsticks — alone each can spear the fried shrimp, but together we can eat the whole meal. Or scissors — Ron's side works for slicing open a package, but my help is necessary for cutting out shapes. With chopsticks and scissors, each part has a role. That's why you have to buy left-handed scissors if you're left handed. They only work a certain way.

You would be hard pressed to pinpoint Ron's leadership in our marriage, especially if your picture of leadership requires that one be "in charge" in every area. Or if your picture puts the husband in the role of benevolent dictator — king even — sitting in his favorite chair issuing directives.

However, Ron and I both know he's in the leadership position. He just doesn't have to prove it all the time for it to be so. God has given us an order in marriage and the family. It's an order that expects equality — equality in respect, in value, in importance, in influence — but it's still an order. Even with chopsticks and scissors there's an efficient, and an inefficient, way to use them.

Leadership in our marriage, and I think in the biblical picture as well, is a *foundation*. It's a core value that influences how we look at our family, but it's not always obvious in our behavior.

A Leadership Comeback

Today the men who attend Christian retreats and rallies are encouraged to be leaders, yes, but servants at heart. Leaders who put the other people in their lives first, before themselves. Leaders who elevate the dreams of their wives and children before their own. When these men examine the needs of their wives, they're coming up with words like *respect, equality, love, listening, value, honor*. They want to begin uplifting their wives in a way that preserves, not demeans, their dignity, uniqueness, individuality, and their necessity as valuable contributors to society.

Jeff and Claire married after living together several years. They brought rocky pasts and plenty of mistakes into their marriage. On their wedding day Claire again heard words about God that she had buried since childhood. They made her think, and she became a Christian not long after that. Soon she realized that she and Jeff had nothing in common spiritually. They drew apart. But about six months later, miraculously and unexpectedly, Jeff accepted Christ.

Jeff decided to attend a Promise Keepers' rally in Detroit. He learned about godly, servant-like leadership. "When he came home, he took me by the hand," says Claire, "drew me down to kneel beside him on the floor, and prayed over me. He was so tender and so loving. He prayed that the hurt and pain of my past would go away. It was the turning point in my being able to trust men again."

Jeff and Claire's story is not unique. Remember the money hassle between Bill and Ginny? Bill's accountability group and his association with Promise Keepers helped save their marriage. His friends talked him through the issue, helped him see the truth, and, more importantly, helped him shape his attitudes about money. Now he's paying Ginny for her work and has added her name to all of his accounts.

These couples represent very positive changes in home leadership. Many Christian men today are re-examining manhood and its practical outworkings and are trying to shoulder some of their wives' burdens, to be more involved with their children, and to initiate strong spiritual lives. Godly leadership is making a comeback. For some couples it's a smooth, easy ride; for others it means a seemingly never-ending adjustment.

With the Queen's Help

Change is hard, and significant change — moving away from years of wrong patterns — is harder. We cannot pretend that a weekend in the stadium is all it takes.

Encouraging our husbands to be the men and the leaders God has created them to be is one of our most important, and difficult, tasks. "It's a delicate balance," says Barbara Rainey, "of being a helpmate without usurping his leadership. When you adapt to your husband, you grant him the freedom to lead you and your family and make it easier for him to follow God."[3]

The helper status can be understood in the simple task of making beds. When you and your daughter make *her* bed, you are helping her. When you and your daughter are making *your* bed, she is helping you. What makes the difference? The helper position has nothing to do with ability, lesser rights, or inferiority. It has everything to do with who is responsible for making that bed.

"It is a special calling to come alongside a man, to adapt to him, and to help him become all God intended," Barbara says. "It is a privilege that should not be demeaned."[4]

Bringing Back the King

So how is this biblical leadership played out day by day? It can't always be reduced to a few steps or a formula, but it is helpful to hear how other women have adapted to the challenge. How does a queen go about trying to change the order of the kingdom's rule? How does she hand over responsibility for the kingdom and its subjects? Harder still, what if she already thinks the king controls too much himself?

Following are some tips for a smoother transfer of leadership:

Let him stumble here or there. John and Giselle have been married seventeen years and have three teenage daughters. Just in the last three years John has become involved with a small group, has been to several Promise Keepers' rallies, and is working through a Bible study that is helping him define his role as a husband and father.

Giselle's struggle has been to let John lead. "After all," she says, "he picked me as his wife because he knew I'd take control, take over for him." Poor male role models in his past convinced John that he should take a backseat in leadership. Giselle went along with it. She was a good leader, so she assumed the role, disciplining the girls, handling the finances, telling John when to mow the lawn, and making sure he got to work on time.

When John began to see the need to take on responsibility, Giselle began to see that each time she took over for John, she was interfering with any lesson God might have for him. For Giselle to step back did not require her tossing her abilities out the window — but only setting them aside for a time to allow her husband to grow in those areas, too.

Keep using your strengths. A man's leadership of the family shouldn't presume that he's capable or even needs to have *more* say in *every* area of family management. In order to lead our families intelligently, our husbands *need* our input, convictions, opinions, and ideas.

Ron is vitally interested in our children's education. Until college entered the picture, however, I did the research and decided what schools they'd attend. With both parents' support, they've done it all — from private to public to home school.

One spring, when a change was needed for the following fall, I was really in a turmoil about school. Christian or public? We had several choices, and, believe me, I interrogated nearly every parent I knew about our decision. We were getting close to the wire, and nothing was clear to me. All along Ron had said "public." But still I stewed, questioned, and prayed, waiting for an inner conviction and assurance that what Ron said was right.

Finally one morning in my quiet time I laid it all out, told God I'd done all the research, made all the pro/con lists, and prayed diligently for months. "You've got to tell me today," I told Him.

"Listen to your husband," I sensed God say.

This made sense to me and was a relief as well. I decided to agree with Ron's judgment, as head of the family, about the situation and send the kids to public school. *That's* when God showed me a confirming Scripture that verified what Ron had said all along.

While still working interdependently and in light of our understanding of biblical leadership, together Ron and I exercised our particular strengths and level of involvement. We came up with an answer that met our children's needs, addressed our concerns, and respected our individual ways of coming to conclusions.

Accept underleaders and overleaders. So what's a wife to do if her husband doesn't act like much of a servant-leader — and he doesn't mind? Many, many women are in that category. Our husbands rarely line up in the middle of the road. We may be married to an "underleader" or an "overleader." What does that require of us? How does our response scoot our husbands closer to that middle line?

Somehow we have to remember that in biblical leadership, men have been given the task of leading their wives and families by the God who created them, who knows them, and us, inside and out. We limit God by requiring that His leaders all look alike.

Recently I asked Giselle, "What does good husband leadership look like?" She must have done a lot of thinking about it because she shared some specific insights.

"He would have a general awareness of what's going on in the family — physically, spiritually, mentally, emotionally, financially," she began. "He would be a man of prayer, interceding daily for his family. He's the first line of defense. He would be willing to be the front man spiritually. He needs to be able to read the climate of the home. And if he's not good at that, he should take counsel from his wife, like a boss or a general does."

Giselle went on to describe a leader who would be willing to set short- and long-range goals for his children and be ready and prepared to deal with situations, such as the dating issue, when they arise. He would be willing to learn what he doesn't know. "Servant leadership requires a constant learning curve, just doing and learning about what needs to be done — even if it's meeting a need by playing Barbies on the floor."

That's a good answer — and a tall order! I wonder what a husband would answer if asked about leading the ideal wife? How would he describe that wife?

If you're not sure about your husband's desires and expectations in this arena, why not ask him? "Honey, do you feel like the leader here? What does that mean to you? How can I help? What areas would you like to change or have more say over if you felt I would cooperate with your suggestions?"

Every man who has turned his heart toward God is walking potential. God wants His men to be good leaders. If you believe this, and that God will work with the raw potential He designed, you will create a safe atmosphere in which your husband can change. We can give our husbands no greater gift as they learn to be God's kind of leaders than to accept them for who they are — and who they aren't, yet.

Endure conflicts with grace. One thing we can be sure of in life is difficulty. Whether they realize it or not, undoubtedly a large number of couples' conflicts revolve around the issue of leadership. Who has final say? Who is right?

How can you handle these conflicts in a way that's filled with grace and, yet, doesn't neglect your duty to give input?

If your husband is an overleader...

• Show respect for your husband's opinion, even when you disagree with his conclusion. One way to do this is by validating his course of logic. "I can see why you think it's best for Billy to stay at Mom's. After all, he..." When your husband feels that you understand his reasoning, he may feel less pressure to prove his case and be more open to your ideas.

• Be careful not to attack his moral character or his position of leadership.

• Look for calm moments when you can have a reasonable discussion about how his behaviors make you feel.

• Watch out for a competitive spirit.

If your husband is an underleader...

• Help him see that responsibility not personality is the determining factor in leadership. He can be a great leader no matter what his temperament, education, or background.

• Give your husband opportunities to lead. In other words, give up a little of your territory. Most likely, things won't fall apart right away, if at all.

• Encourage every single strength you see, and look for more.

• Model leadership behavior that includes challenging him at times but also showing respect for his position.

A Fairy Tale Ending?

Remember our king and our queen? When our king put his crown back on, there was a collective sigh of relief from the women in the kingdom. Just the act of looking like a leader sent a message to the other men that they, too, might want to make some changes. Slowly but surely strength returned to the men, and thereby to the families, and in turn to the kingdom.

Their wives? They didn't feel displaced at all, much to their own surprise. They were, however, glad to get that heavy armor off. And when our queen gave that crown and that position back to her husband, she didn't retire to her needlepoint, as some might suggest. She reorganized the knights-in-training program and exchanged her square dining table for a round one.

And then, did the king and queen live happily ever after? It's a question we can't help asking. Take a minute and think about "happy ever after." It suggests a guaranteed future full of joy, love, acceptance, peace. But don't wait for your "happy ever after" to come in one eternal lump. These qualities exist in marriage, but they happen one day at a time, to couples who are partners in promise.

In the next few chapters we'll be looking at other important principles for couples in the midst of change: forgiving the past, loving in the present, and trusting for the future. By knowing such keys, all kings and queens have the potential for happiness.

Promising Conversations

Ephesians 4:1–6 — *"I, therefore, the prisoner of the Lord, entreat you to walk in a manner worthy of the calling with which you have been called, with all humility and gentleness, with patience, showing forbearance to one another in love, being diligent to preserve the unity of the Spirit in the bond of peace.*

"There is one body and one Spirit, just as also you were called in one hope of your calling; one Lord, one faith, one baptism, one God and Father of all who is over all and through all and in all."

1. Do you walk in humility in your home?

   Are you gentle?

   Are you generally patient?

   Do you show forbearance (self-control, endurance, mercy)?

   Do you preserve or destroy unity?

   Is your home peaceful?

2. Leadership/headship in marriage is the aspect that elicits the most discussion and argument when the subject of marriage comes up. Why do you think this is so?

3. In what areas do you find it difficult to relinquish or share control?

4. How is leadership in your marriage handled differently than it was in your parents' marriage?

5. The Greek word for submission is *hupotasso*, which means "to place oneself under a leader to ensure victory in battle." It has nothing to do with weakness, subservience, or passivity. Think of your own analogy that best describes your marriage. Are you an example of a relay team — or of a spectator sport?

Private Consideration

Read Ephesians 5:15–33 and note the entire context of these well-known verses on marriage. Note particularly verses 15–21 and the emphasis both on making the most of your time and on the mutual subjection of husband and wife. *This* is the model.

1. How do you emotionally react to the idea of submission?

2. How do you want to deal with submission in your marriage? Work on and write down a definition/description of biblical leadership. (For example, "When a man is leading his family, he...")

3. How do you think your husband views submission? Does he understand it the same way you do?

To love is not to view someone as being the most wonderful person in the world or to think of them as a saint. On the contrary, it may mean to see them as we must come to see ourselves, even as the "chief of sinners." It is to see all their weakness, their falseness and shoddiness, to have all their very worst habits exposed — and then to be enabled, by the pure grace of God not only to accept them, but to accept them in a deeper way than was ever before possible.... Before love can really begin to be love, it must face and forgive the very worst in the person loved

MIKE MASON

CHAPTER SEVEN

Choices of the Heart

J anie and Chris have been married fifteen years. Chris is a rather stoic man who doesn't talk much, and whose wife wishes he did. Lately, however, Chris has begun to come out of his shell a bit. At a recent CrossTrainers retreat in Des Moines, he learned more about the importance of sharing his life and feelings with Janie.

So one night after dinner Chris began to open up about several things in his past he had been reluctant to tell Janie. In his desire for oneness he confessed a *lot* — and scared his wife. Now Janie has to deal with new, unsettling knowledge about Chris's past in addition to the upheavals that naturally occur when a husband attempts to change.

What does it really mean to live as a partner with a changing, imperfect, promising man? What guiding principles will help us to encourage our husbands long term?

We start with the past — not to dwell on it, or live in it, or figure it all out — but because it colors what's going on in our marriages today.

Ironically a man's steps of progress toward the future can often trigger resentment about the past.

Dealing with the past is crucial to building a great future on a clean slate. Unresolved issues, buried conflicts, and, most of all, unforgiveness can tangle up any couple's best efforts to become partners in promise. In fact, most of the time we're unaware of just how deeply the past is causing us to stumble through our current lives.

Georgia spent several years getting over Jeff's disrespectful treatment of her father right after they married. At least she *thought* she was over it. But the other night when Jeff was teaching their children about kind ways to say things, Georgia remembered with sudden clarity the unkind words Jeff had spoken to her father. Pretending to read a magazine, she sat through the rest of the evening immersed in old hurts.

Here's another common scenario: Christine and Tim married young. During their rocky first years, Tim carried on a family history of verbal and physical abuse in their marriage. Through God's tender work in his life, Tim later made an about-face and asked Christine for forgiveness. Things improved quickly — until one night Tim blew it and yelled at Christine. Within an hour he tearfully apologized, but she struggled to respond. Her mind kept going over a long list of previous violations, with this new one added on.

Both cases call for the single, but perhaps most difficult, choice of the heart: forgiveness. So simple to say, yet so hard to carry out — especially when the pain has deepened through the years.

The Face of Forgiveness

Leonardo da Vinci was a tremendously gifted man. An astronomer, architect, botanist, biologist, artist, engineer, inventor — there were few academic and artistic disciplines in which he didn't dabble. Perhaps because his ideas and inventions were so radical for his time, he wrote some of his notes left-handed and backwards. One of his notebooks recorded "EVOM TON SEOD NUS EHT." But da Vinci's giftedness came with a short temper.

While painting *The Last Supper* in about 1495, da Vinci got into a serious quarrel with another artist. What better retribution than to give Judas, the betrayer of Christ, the face of his foe. So he did. As the painting neared completion, all that was left was the face of Jesus. Day after day he drew faces. But no matter how hard he worked, da Vinci couldn't get Jesus' countenance right — until he forgave the other artist. Once that relationship was mended, da Vinci had the freedom of heart to finish his now famous painting.

Like da Vinci, neither we nor our husbands have freedom to move ahead — to complete the works of our lives — until we can truly paint the face of forgiveness. The Bible puts it this way: "And be kind to one another, tender-hearted, forgiving each other, just as God in Christ also has forgiven you" (Ephesians 4:32).

Thankfully, God sees us not as *compared* to Christ, but as *covered* by Christ. It's an amazing concept that leaves me breathless when I think about it. He forgives us unconditionally, regardless of what we do. He forgives us repetitively, no matter how many times we mess up. He forgives us completely, never mentioning our sins again, even though we might. And He forgives us eagerly, longing to restore our relationship.

That's the good news. Now here's the hard news. This is the same forgiveness He asks us to bestow on our changing, growing husbands. Only He doesn't really ask us, as in "Would you please do this?" He commands it, as in "Forgive." It's not an option from His point of view.

Forgiveness for something that happened in the past doesn't mean glossing over offenses, ignoring hurt and pain, or stuffing feelings. In fact, true forgiveness demands the wrongs be brought to light in order to restore the honesty and openness of the relationship. The healing of the relationship is the goal. And that means choosing to deal with the tough stuff, as difficult as that can be.

Forgiveness is often difficult because we don't realize what it means —
we give it an incomplete definition. Neil Anderson in his book *The Bondage
Breaker* gets past the glibness of "Sure, I forgive you" to its reality. "Forgiveness is agreeing to live with the consequences of another person's sin." Now
that's a mouthful of truth!

"Forgiveness is costly," he says. "We pay the price of the evil we forgive.
Yet you're going to live with those consequences whether you want to or not;
your only choice is whether you will do so in the bitterness of unforgiveness
or the freedom of forgiveness.... Forgiveness deals with your pain, not
another's behavior."[1]

Forgiveness is a choice of the heart you make to release your husband
and yourself to grow. In fact, you alone may hold the key to his future right
there in the palm of the past. But just how does a wife unlock the doors of
her heart, and her husband's, to let forgiveness in?

Journey toward Forgiveness

Interestingly enough, the Hebrew word we translate "forgive" in the Old
Testament is used solely of God. It doesn't refer, in any of its forms, to people
forgiving one another.

But in the New Testament, after Pentecost, when the Holy Spirit began
indwelling believers, forgiving one another does enter the picture of obedience. The difference is that we now have the power within us to do it! Never
before was that possible. Forgiveness is a divine act. For us to forgive completely implies the necessity of walking in the Spirit moment by moment, of
being frequently aware of our relationship with God and how we're handling
our own sin.

I'm so encouraged by Philippians 1:6: "being confident of this, that he
who began a good work in you will carry it on to completion until the day
of Christ Jesus" (NIV). The burden is not on our shoulders alone, but also
on those of Jesus Himself. However, until that day when we all are forgiven

forever, we would do well to remind ourselves of practical ways to be for-giving.

Your husband's side is your side. One of the hardest things about our hus-band's mistakes is that so often they directly affect our own lives. We are intricately bound together, and when he chooses sin or insensitivity, we *both* pay the consequences. Instead of working together on problems with the help of forgiveness, a standoff takes place. The couple imagines themselves to be against each other — on separate sides.

Sometimes forgiveness just can't take place until one partner agrees to come over and *join the other's side,* even if that partner is in sin. My dear friend Elizabeth recently called with the satisfying news that she and her husband, Jimmy, are finally recovering from his alcohol addiction. For years they had quietly borne a burden of guilt, secrecy, and anger. The "he's the problem/she's the victim" mentality was pushing them apart and setting up their children for a difficult future.

Elizabeth took the first step, initiating several tough-love measures that put change in motion. Then they broke their silence, admitting their struggles to a few carefully chosen friends and subsequently to a counselor. Now they're finally on the road to forgiveness and healing.

Jimmy and Elizabeth have changed *together,* not in the same ways, but through the same situation. Jimmy has resolutely dealt with his past and his predisposition. In many ways he was freed from his inertia when Elizabeth came alongside and faced the problem with him, realizing that her criticism had not been constructive. She chose to replace her anger and reproach with praise and a conscious choice not to judge anymore.

Elizabeth took joint ownership of his problem, and that has made all the difference. She told me, "He's fallen in love with me all over again."

Coming alongside our husbands when they've committed major offenses is possible, especially when we're willing to recognize our capacity for sin and need for forgiveness. I try to remember two truths: Forgiveness is difficult, but God nonetheless commands it. With those two premises, says Nancy Swihart, we can echo her prayer in *Beside Every Great Dad*. "Lord, create in me the freedom to forgive, and enable me to do that which is unnatural for me."[2]

Forgiveness is a daily friend. Large, seemingly unforgivable acts or habits are one thing, but everyday life is another. To forgive a huge, painful event from long ago sometimes feels easier than to forgive the daily wounds we inflict on one another. It won't be enough to pull the "big gun" of forgiveness out of the closet once a year. For your marriage to thrive, forgiveness must become a close companion, a ready friend. If our husbands fail to keep new promises, our readiness to forgive will help them decide whether to try again and again — or not.

Elizabeth describes her struggle with daily forgiving this way: "The very power that lifted Jesus from the grave is also able to help me do the right thing. There are times when I just stop and I pray *that*...."

As much as God is a part of forgiving our changing husbands, we can't ignore our responsibility. Whenever we're faced with a hurt, we have that choice. Nancy Swihart says, "When you are tempted to nurse a hurt and bear a grudge, you are tempted by a lie. The lie behind the temptation is that this grudge will restore some iota of your joy by granting you power over the person who has hurt you. Supposedly, you have the power to punish him by withholding your care and concern. You have the power to stop hurting because you've replaced the pain with anger."[3]

Recently Ron and I faced an issue that was painful to me largely because I had to account for my own wrong. When I finally acknowledged the need to deal with the situation, my first feeling was heaviness, the kind that makes you feel you just gained ten pounds. I remember walking around the school track behind our house, concentrating on his wrong, my wrong, letting the gravity of it all weigh me down.

"Mary," I said to myself, "you've been a Christian for twenty-seven years.

You know the routine you need to go through when you're troubled. Don't put it off!"

So I acknowledged God as sovereign, loving, all-knowing, and wanting our best; admitted and confessed my fear, my sin, my reluctance to act in a mature way; prayed for my husband's response and my words to ask forgiveness; and thought through the timing.

Letting go is good to do. Now that we've come alongside and owned part of the problem, even if all we needed to own was our response, it's time to set offenses aside. That doesn't necessarily mean forgetting what's happened, but it does mean choosing not to live in its shadow or power anymore.

Ted and Katie's courtship could hardly be called pristine. As new Christians, they lacked sexual vigilance in their time together. Though they felt guilty, neither could shut the door of sexuality they'd opened. Now, after many years of marriage, their sexual relationship is suffering, in part because of a deep-seated need to deal completely with their premarital relationship.

When confronting her marriage problems, Katie was challenged to increase her transparency with Ted and to encourage his transparency with her. As they talked, they realized that the guilt from their past relationship was affecting their present one. Looking back they saw how unresolved blame and guilt kept them from intimacy in all areas of their marriage.

There comes a point in all of our relationships, but particularly our marriages, when choosing to set things aside, out of the way where they belong, becomes important. The past is past. Even when past actions have had horrific consequences, we eventually have to cease living in their power. God is in control.

We have a choice — to retaliate with punishment, thereby prolonging our own pain, or to forgive without strings, which lets everybody off the hook. Norm Wright says forgiveness can be like a tug-of-war. The struggle continues only as long as two sides pull the rope. If one of you lets go — forgives, relaxes, accepts — the struggle is over.

I suspect massive changes would occur in our marriages if we could just leave that rope on the ground.

Choosing to set aside an event in order to forgive is a mature thing to do. It makes change a challenge, instead of a setback. It's the kind of taking control of one's life that is healthy and energizing. Forgiving the past puts what we want to get rid of behind us and frees us up to the work of the present.

Life-Giving Apologies

Sometimes what starts as an apology can end up as an even more intense argument. The art of forgiving and asking forgiveness in a way that doesn't reflect negatively on the other person or inflame the situation is a learned one. And when it's learned successfully, it reveals a humble spirit that's hard to ignore. Here are some tips. (All these tips will work better if you pray first.)

Giving Forgiveness

- Thank your husband for his honesty and apology.
- Give him your full attention, eye contact, and time to finish.
- Give him a specific answer. "I forgive you for _____."
- If possible, express belief in his good intentions.
- Avoid bringing up his wrong or your hurt again.
- Express love to close the gap between you.

Asking Forgiveness

- Don't phrase your apology in terms that transfer blame to the other person or his feelings. "I'm sorry you got mad at me."
- Admit your wrong in specific terms. "I was wrong when I _____. Please forgive me."
- Don't qualify your apology. "I'm sorry, but you..."

- Choose your timing. Sometimes your husband will need a little cooling off time before he really hears your heart. Sometimes you need a little as well.
- Rehearse your words and your body language. A big offense needs a big rehearsal.
- Acknowledge and validate his hurt feelings: "I can understand how that would upset you."
- Let him answer your apology in his own time.
- Express your love.

Staying One Step Ahead

Changing circumstances, changing priorities, changing values, changing habits — all of these turnarounds need to happen in an environment of acceptance. Hand in hand with forgiving a husband, in fact one step ahead of it, comes acceptance — an ongoing state of love and nonjudgment. "Accept one another, then, just as Christ accepted you, in order to bring praise to God" (Romans 15:7, NIV).

Eleanor grew up in the formal Northeast, outside of Boston. She attended college in Colorado and met Matt, a free-spirited westerner who captivated her rigid heart. Matt's spontaneity attracted her before they were married and into the early months after their wedding. But soon after, Eleanor woke up to whom and what she'd married. Could she accept him?

Matt's vexing habits, like swinging his booted feet up onto the coffee table or leaving the toilet seat up, were nothing compared to his tobacco chewing. Eleanor despised it. It topped the ever-increasing list of changes she wanted to see in Matt.

One day at a men's retreat he finally did start to change. He recommitted himself to loving Eleanor unconditionally; he recommitted himself to God and to the men in his church. So many areas of his life were in a positive upheaval, his head was spinning. Eleanor, however, didn't see those changes as clearly as she saw his feet, the toilet seat, and his tobacco. Those were the things she harped on.

Matt couldn't believe it. He thought he was becoming what Eleanor wanted and needed, but she kept measuring him by her lifestyle preference. She was allowing little things about Matt to cloud the important growth he was going through. His changes were unimportant to her because she hadn't yet accepted Matt for who he was.

Pastor/counselor Bob Hicks says in *Uneasy Manhood*, "Every man sooner or later must face the reality that his wife will never be totally pleased with him."[4] Is that really what they're feeling — or what wives communicate?

I guess it's human nature not to be totally pleased with anyone else. By our actions it seems what we really want is someone just like us. In fact, you may be hoping the changes your husband is going through will make him just like you. But we need our husbands to be who they are. That's why God put us together. We enrich each other's lives like crayons add depth and interest to a coloring book.

One goal of marriage is to establish that safe place where we're not afraid to be uncovered, in every sense of the word, before the other. A safe place where we're known and we know another person more deeply than anyone else, where we're unconditionally accepted. Only then will change feel less threatening and become encouraging and safe.

I can't know what areas are the hardest to accept in your marriage. Does your husband go out with friends too much? Does he not enjoy your hobbies? Does he have obnoxious habits and weaknesses?

That Really Bugs Me

Perhaps the biggest lesson we all need to learn is how to be a student of our spouses. The changes they're going through are just refining who they already are, not eliminating the person inside.

Elisabeth Elliot puts it this way: "Your husband is known fully only to

God, and stands in a sense alone before Him. God said to Abraham, 'Walk before Me and be thou perfect.' He did not suggest that Abraham could walk before Sarah and be perfect. Ultimately he is God's man. He is free, and you must always reverence this freedom."[5]

Ron and I have very different personalities. Every now and then I get tired of his sunny outlook, always seeing the best *and* diffusing my annoyance with humor. I'd like to have a few more serious discussions. But I need his buoyancy and spontaneity and risk-taking to encourage my own. It's a challenge to live together, but a good one.

Our backgrounds are just as different as our personalities. I'll never forget the day my father sat me down on his bed, with the door closed, and encouraged me to get Ron to stop wearing "those tacky, polyester leisure suits." We've both changed throughout our twenty-six-year marriage: some of that change comes from blending part of our backgrounds and accepting the rest.

Accepting our husbands, with all they bring into our marriages and all they will become as they change into the image of God, means that we *have* to overlook some things and accept others. There's no getting around it.

"Why is unconditional acceptance so important?" Dennis and Barbara Rainey ask in *Building Your Mate's Self-Esteem*. "Because if you accept only in part, you can love only in part. And if you love in part, your mate's self-esteem will never be complete. That area of rejection will keep your mate from becoming all he was meant to be."[6]

To accept what our past has made us, and to forgive the hurts, isn't part of a magic fix-all formula — but they are choices our hearts can make that will free us to handle today.

Promising Conversations

Ephesians 4:31–5:2 — *"Let all bitterness and wrath and anger and clamor and slander be put away from you, along with all malice. And be kind to one another, tender-hearted, forgiving each other, just as God in Christ also has forgiven you.*

"Therefore be imitators of God, as beloved children; and walk in love, just as Christ also loved you, and gave Himself up for us, an offering and a sacrifice to God as a fragrant aroma."

1. Think about a specific area or incident when you were forgiven (by God, your husband, etc.).

2. How can you apply the above scripture when you feel wronged? Can you think of an example?

We all have idiosyncrasies — peculiar or particular ways of doing things. A good marriage necessitates accepting things in the other person that might irritate us.

3. What are some of your husband's idiosyncrasies? How do you respond to them? With acceptance? With irritation?

4. Which of those would become endearing memories if he were absent?

Private Considerations

Going beyond idiosyncrasies, think through traits or characteristics in your husband that hold a bit more weight (such as personality).

1. What trait(s) do you need to learn to accept in your husband?

2. What traits are hard for your husband to accept in you?

Purposeful giving is not apt to deplete one's resources; it belongs to that natural order of giving that seems to renew itself even in the act of depletion. The more one gives, the more one has to give — like milk in the breast.

ANNE MORROW LINDBERGH

CHAPTER EIGHT

Love Covers a Lot of Stuff

Nancy works the night shift as a cardiac nurse, arriving home about the time her three children leave for school. Her husband, Rick, is a high school math teacher and coach, currently laid off because of budget cuts. These days Rick fills in the gaps at home, including getting the kids ready for school. He really tries hard to remember it all — teeth brushed, matching socks, lunches, signed permission slips, homework, show-and-tell days. This part of his routine is definitely out of his comfort zone, but he knows it's necessary, and he does his best.

What irritates Nancy are the little mistakes Rick makes — sending lunches with too much sugar, not checking the homework, forgetting the permission slips altogether. Can't he get organized the night before or make a morning checklist? After all, *she* used to get it all done.

Then one day Nancy looked beyond the candy wrappers in the lunch bags and saw the defeated expression on Rick's face. That's when she realized how important it was for her to honor Rick's *efforts*, not just his *successes*. Now she looks for ways to honor him — by complimenting him, by appreciating and thanking him, by respecting his way of doing things. Nancy's learning that love really does cover a lot of stuff. The question is, what feels like love to a husband? How exactly does your husband hear you rooting for him in the thick of things?

A Blanket of Honor

When asked, most husbands agree on one thing that they desire from their wives more than any other — honor. "My wife wants flowers and dinners out," said one man, "but what I want most is for her to honor me, to respect me, to look up to me."

What is honor exactly? Honor esteems the humanity of a person, the position of a person, even if actions are not always honorable. It gets at the heart of what it means to be created in the image of God. It separates the action from the actor, the sin from the sinner.

"Be devoted to one another in brotherly love. Honor one another above yourselves" (Romans 12:10, NIV). To cast a loving blanket of honor over your husband in the midst of tumultuous changes is a powerful statement to him — and to the rest of the world.

Although honor is a choice, it's not always easy. Elevating another person above ourselves, as Romans 12 encourages us to do, is unnatural. Or rather, it's *super*-natural. It is a rich challenge, with a huge payoff. One way to better understand how honoring is actually lived out is to look at the meanings of the words *deference* and *preference*.

The Beauty of Deference

Deference is a synonym for *reverence, veneration,* and *esteem*. My dictionary also says it "implies a courteous yielding...of one's own judgment, opinion... to that of another." Deference is an attitude you take. It's putting another person first. It's a sign of character, not compromise.

Hardly a woman has crossed my path who doesn't have a story about driving. Here's a typical one. Rob and Deborah had their camping trip all planned. Actually Rob let Deborah plan it; he got the car in supreme working order and bought a bunch of camping stuff. They only had a few days of vacation but wanted to spend it at the same campsite where they'd honeymooned five years before. This meant driving a fair distance. Rob was in charge of the directions.

They got off on time with their two boys and all their paraphernalia — diapers, bottles, toys, clothes — packed in tight around the camping gear and food. If they didn't make too many stops, they'd arrive by dusk. Everything went according to plan until late afternoon. Rob couldn't quite remember which exit to take off the freeway. The exit's name reminded him of someone in his family, he recalled, but he just couldn't think of who it was.

The exit coming up was Thomas Drive. He had an Uncle Tom. But that wasn't it. Garland Avenue was next. He had a sister named Judy. Judy Garland? No.

"Where's the map, honey?" Deborah asked when she noticed the concerned look on his face.

There was no map. Rob had left it on the counter by the phone. But he knew he would recognize the area when they got to it. So they kept driving.

Deborah will tell you exactly at what point she was ready to get out of the car to hitchhike home. But Rob didn't give up until nine o'clock when it was pitch dark and the boys were out cold. Deborah had said some things that intensified the cold temperature in the car. Why couldn't Rob have simply asked someone for directions?

She's not sure what checked her perspective, but she noticed that Rob was feeling miserable. She reached across in the dark and gently massaged his shoulders. "It's okay, honey. Let's just get a motel room." At the nearest Holiday Inn, they carried their kids and the necessaries inside and quietly made love under the covers.

The next morning Rob had no defensive walls to take down. He'd been shown honor as a person and a husband, in spite of his mistake. He asked directions, and everyone enjoyed lunch on the picnic table in their old campsite.

In the midst of an irritating time, Deborah grasped that there's a difference between deference and subservience. God asks us to live deferentially with one another. He doesn't call us, even under the Ephesians 5 discussion of submission, to subjugate our intellect or our personhood to anyone. Even our obedience to Him keeps intact our freedom of choice.

So why is deference so difficult? Why isn't it the first thing we consider? Because deference to another often means giving up control. This just isn't in our nature, particularly as we see changes taking place in our husbands. We want to influence the direction they're going. More often than not, we're pretty sure we've been there ourselves and know what worked for us.

Deference makes you ask: Does my desire to control indicate that I don't trust God? Will yielding control help my husband's growth or encourage him? Is this control issue worth a fight? Deference keeps us from battling over the smallest things — which route to church, which restaurant, which television show, who gets the remote control.

While traveling this summer, I spent one night at a bed-and-breakfast with my daughter, a friend, and her two daughters. We sat around the breakfast table on our departure day with several couples we'd met the night before. Our conversation turned to this guy thing of hogging the remote control. Each man at the table acknowledged his reluctance to part with that little bit of power; each wife nodded her head and rolled her eyes.

Ron and I have the same problem. But one night, after we had just hooked up a new TV, he changed the channel with his remote, and I changed it back with mine. The battle was on. We laughed, and finally I gave up. It wasn't worth it. And you know, it really wasn't. It's perfectly all right for me to remind Ron that I'm interested in a particular program, but it's usually not a battle I need to win.

How does a wife show deference to her husband? By not interfering with his choices, unless truly necessary. By respecting his efforts to grow. By not trying to influence his male way of doing things. By not always expecting *him* to defer.

The Power of Preference

A second way to honor is to show preference to our husbands. Practically speaking, preference means giving someone our focused attention and affection. Aside from our relationship with Him, God set one relationship above all others — the relationship between a husband and wife. It's the reason we leave our parents. It's the relationship that continues after our children leave home. It's the relationship that best represents Christ with His church. And it requires our preference.

I've begun to think of preference as a rubber band. At times a child's school struggles, a parent's illness, or moving to a new house can pull our attention in another direction. But when the needy time is over, the focus of our preference should come back into place, back to our husbands.

For me, preference means making time for Ron, really listening when he needs to dream out loud. It means stocking the fridge with Diet Snapple, making the coffee every night before we go to bed, and using Miracle Whip instead of mayonnaise. It means, after twenty-six years I'd better figure out how to make that great crab cocktail his mom made for Thanksgiving. That kind of attention to detail conveys honor to our husbands.

If your husband is just now trying to make a spiritual difference in his life and thereby in your marriage, he's probably extra sensitive to the level of your attention — the kind of attention that says, "You are important to me. What you're learning is important to me, too, because you are my husband."

Ron has been a line-dancing fan ever since it hit the culture. But for some reason, the enthusiasm for "grapevines" has passed me by. His keeps growing. He's got a cowboy hat and boots and now some video instruction tapes. It's grabbing him hard.

I realized how hard one Tuesday when he called from his car phone around noon. "Hey, honey, there's a line-dancing class at the community center at two o'clock. How about going with me?"

I wondered, silently, who could make a class at that time. And even as I reluctantly answered, "I guess so," I began ticking off the reasons why I didn't want to go. I didn't want to interrupt my day. I didn't want to admit I couldn't do this stuff. I didn't even want to learn how to do it. I just flat out didn't want to go.

Now I had to drop everything and get ready. But it was such a small thing to do. Why did it feel so hard? I prayed, asking God to change my attitude. And hurry! I had to be there in twenty minutes. Only then did I feel my tightened spirit relax, and although I wasn't excited about it, I was ready to go.

So in we marched to this class. I suspected we wouldn't run into couples our age, and sure enough, one peek through the doors revealed seven gray-haired women in orthopedic shoes, along with the instructor. Ron looked at me, and I looked at him. We probably should have stayed. It would have been about my speed. But we didn't. I mean, we still have those video-tapes....

Going along now and then with things our husbands love, or at least trying them out, is a way for us to show our husbands we prefer them above all others. And who knows, maybe one day I'll learn how to do a "grapevine" and like it.

The Languages of Love

Since we're talking about creating an atmosphere of love and honor, we can't let sex go unmentioned. It would be a mistake not to acknowledge that lovemaking gives our husbands assurance. When they're making an effort to turn around spiritually, much of their lives is in upheaval. Our holding steady in this very tangible area of affection is of immense comfort. It communicates a security that our love is stable even as they work through changes.

Besides lovemaking, we can discover what we can do or say that communicates "I love you" to our husbands. Dr. Gary Chapman, in his stimulating book *The Five Love Languages*, introduces us to the five primary and practical ways we receive and give love. Finding the primary love language of our husbands, and how to express it, gives a wife tools she can use daily in her marriage. These tools take the deference and preference we talked about and give them feet and hands.

Here are brief descriptions of Dr. Chapman's targeted languages:

- Quality Time — where focused conversation and attention is most important.
- Words of Affirmation — where verbal appreciation and affirmation are most necessary.
- Gifts — where little gifts of love, regardless of cost, demonstrate love.
- Acts of Service — where love is best expressed by serving one another.
- Physical touch — where frequent pats, hugs, and shoulder rubs communicate love.[1]

My husband loves bringing the kids and me gifts from his frequent travels. When our son and daughter were small, he collected all sorts of little hotel soaps and shower caps, airplane souvenir wings and cards — any kind of little memento to stuff in his suitcase. Other times he'd stop off at the grocery store and pick me up one of those prewrapped bunches of daisies and carnations. I appreciated these greatly, but I couldn't figure out why I wasn't jumping with enthusiasm, until I read Chapman's book.

My love language is acts of service. When he washes the windows or stops at the grocery store on his way home, it communicates love to me. My secondary love language is quality time. I *notice* when Ron sits down with me and initiates conversation.

You might think Ron's love language is gifts. But it's not. That's just what he thought I'd appreciate as an expression of love. His primary love language is physical touch. He loves hugs and holding hands. He loves for our daughter to snuggle with him in front of the TV. He particularly likes working at home with me, just so we can physically connect, hand to hand, now and then, throughout the day.

Think through what would say "I honor you, I love you" to your husband. Then ask him if you're right. Do you know his love language? And does he know yours?

A Cup of Encouragement

As honor is one aspect of creating an atmosphere safe for change, encouragement is the other. "Therefore encourage one another and build each other up..." (1 Thessalonians 5:11, NIV).

Change is not an easy exercise for our husbands. It means they're giving something up — a comfort zone, a habit, or both. What will get them moving, starting the race, leaping the hurdles? Not just an encouraging word, but an encouraging *partner*. They need someone to say, "You're good at this. It's the right time. Look how God has prepared you!"

Peter and Maggie have been married fourteen years. They didn't start their family until they were in their late thirties. Peter's a musician, talented in many fields, with an artist's perfectionism and occasional pessimism. Since Peter works out of their home with a recording studio in one of the bedrooms, he helps out with their preschooler on Maggie's workdays and is there when their daughter gets home from third grade.

Peter's income is substantial but sporadic, while Maggie has a steady, eight-to-five job that includes benefits. Recently this has bothered Peter. He's been hearing a lot about what it means to be the provider for his family. He wishes he had a steadier income so Maggie didn't have to work. Sometimes he considers giving up his music to do something more practical and profitable. He's trying to take the lead as provider in his family and not let his natural pessimism affect them.

Because Maggie is sensitive to Peter's growing conviction to lead, she focuses on admiring him for making the most of his talent and for his efforts as a provider. Maggie's a master at it. She's taken Peter off the hook. Peter is getting the message that she loves him with or without change. For an introspective artist, that's a vital message.

Say Something Nice...

The key to encouraging seems to rest in our speech more than in any other part of us. It is our tongue, what the epistle of James metaphorically calls the bit, the rudder, a spark, a fire, with which we can encourage or discourage most effectively. "No man can tame the tongue," James says "It is a restless evil, full of deadly poison. With the tongue we praise our Lord and Father, and with it we curse men, who have been made in God's likeness" (James 3:8–9, NIV).

We can build up our changing husbands by simple words. Asking questions, the kind that require more than a yes or no, is good. Positive comments about little things go a long way. Saying to him, "I respect the steps you're taking, the work that's involved," frees him to keep going. All of our positive words also communicate another message. They say, "I can see God is working in you."

My husband's public testimony acknowledges that he had a pornography shop in his basement when he was a boy. He hung around with the wrong crowd, and it showed. But close to his thirteenth birthday he asked Christ into his heart, and God turned his life around.

Ron's worked hard to put aside this part of his past. And as his wife, I've gained the benefits of his dealing with it. I tell him regularly how grateful I am that he has not allowed it to harm our marriage. It's that kind of building up, admiring, and noting things that communicates encouragement.

Or Don't Say Anything at All

"If you can't say something nice, then don't say anything at all." It's not bad advice our mothers gave us. Even as nice words can encourage, sometimes it's just as important to know when to *stop* talking. Too often we step in quickly with unsolicited advice and actually tear our husbands down. I've certainly done it.

Dave McCombs, National Director of MAN, says, "Men often translate help [or 'suggestions'] in one of three ways:

- She doesn't respect me.
- She doesn't accept me.
- She doesn't love me the way I am."

As women, we easily ask for help, or at least company. It's natural for us to assume our husbands want the same. But when they're trying something new, and we offer advice without their request, we're saying, "You can't do this without me. You're not capable."

Manipulation is another way women have of motivating, but not encouraging, their husbands. "Honey, would you read this Bible story to Eddie before he goes to bed? I think he sleeps better when you read to him." Regardless of how cunning we might feel, I think the secret's out. Now's the time to fight the urge to "help" or to "teach." As our husbands move toward God's spiritual potential in their lives, it's important our words encourage instead of discourage.

When in Public

When Ron and I first noticed each other, as college students, we had an interesting way of showing it. We cut each other down in front of our friends. We made snide, sarcastic remarks to and about the other. I suppose it was a fractured form of flirting. It was funny for a while, until we became more serious. As soon as we woke up to the deeper level of our relationship, we realized we had to treat each other more carefully.

From that rocky beginning, we learned the power of a word spoken in public. We still fight the inclination to correct each other's stories. I still have to watch my tongue when I'm with my friends. It's easy for me to zero in on one of those insignificant irritations of my husband's and blow it up into an animated luncheon topic. How brazen of me to serve him for lunch — to get a laugh or feel close to my friends!

I've had to ask God to forgive the distorted picture of marriage I've presented at times.

Ask yourself these questions: If you were to poll several of your friends on your husband's character, what would they say? What kind of reputation has he acquired through your conversation? You have the power to honor him as your most supportive friend, as your hero — or destroy him completely.

Failure Is Opportunity

As our men grow and change, what does it mean to encourage them in the face of failure? Often it can mean the difference between hope or giving up.

All of us fail, but a person becomes a failure only when he doesn't learn from those failings. Wrong choices, wrong decisions help our husbands make right ones. For us to look at them in the middle of severe weakness and say, "It's all right. I'm still in love with you and want to be a part of your life," is like throwing a life-saving ring to a person floundering in an ocean.

We honor and encourage our husbands based not on their accomplishments, but on their intrinsic worth. Nancy Swihart, in her contribution to *Beside Every Great Dad*, says, "When a man feels inadequate, honor can give him confidence."[2] If you can say to your husband, after you've watched him blow it again, that your respect for him as a man made in the image of God is not tarnished, you have given him an open door through which he can keep moving.

At the funeral of his wife, Jane, Dr. E. V. Hill told about a time as a struggling preacher he unwisely invested his limited savings. One night he came home to a candlelight dinner. Great. But when he went in the bathroom to wash his hands and flipped the light switch, no light came on. E. V. walked around the house, trying switches here and there, and realized the electricity was off. When he asked his wife about it, she began to cry.

"You work so hard, and we're trying," said Jane, "but it's pretty rough. I didn't have quite enough money to pay the light bill. I didn't want you to know about it, so I thought we would just eat by candlelight."

Dr. Hill's voice shook as he shared his wife's words. "She could have said, 'I've never been in this situation before. I was reared in the home of Dr. Caruthers, and we never had our lights cut off.' She could have broken my spirit. She could have ruined me; she could have demoralized me. But instead she said, 'Somehow or another we'll get these lights on. But let's eat tonight by candlelight.'"[3]

Jane Hill was a woman controlled by the Spirit of God at that moment. She built her husband up and believed the best about him, in the midst of failure, in circumstances that many of us would have used for the opposite effect.

Johnny, the husband of my friend Linda, is working hard at being punctual. He's forty years old, yet still has trouble getting himself together, out the door, and where he needs to be on time. So Linda, in her desire to help him, or perhaps in frustration, used to pad his schedule by setting his appointments fifteen minutes earlier than they really were.

Recently Johnny was convicted about his lateness and committed to working on it. Linda was tempted to keep up her padding but decided that would be sending him the wrong message. Some days he does great, but he still blows it occasionally. She's learning to say, "You're really working on your lateness. I can see your progress." And she's letting him grow by his failure even as she tries to encourage him.

We've looked now at forgiving past mistakes and at honoring our husbands day by day as they try to change. In the next chapter we'll discuss another key we can use to create an atmosphere for growth: trust. Love does cover a lot of stuff, but whom do we trust with our future when our whole world, including our husbands, is changing in front of our eyes?

Promising Conversations

Romans 12:10 — *"Be devoted to one another in brotherly love; give preference to one another in honor."*

Ephesians 4:29 — *"Let no unwholesome word proceed from your mouth, but only such a word as is good for edification according to the need of the moment, that it may give grace to those who hear."*

1. What impression do your friends have of your husband, based on your conversations about him and your attitudes about your marriage?

2. How do women manipulate their husbands? Do you have a particular way of doing it? What specific changes could you make to stop it?

3. According to this chapter, what is your love language? Your husband's?

4. Honoring other people has become a lost art, primarily because it flies so squarely in the face of our generation's tendency to self-absorption. In your marriage, what two things could you sacrifice that would communicate honor to your husband?

Private Considerations

Honor and encouragement have a twofold benefit. They play a huge part in the health of individuals around us, and they keep us from being "hardened by the deceitfulness of sin."

> Hebrews 3:12–13 — *"Take care, brethren, lest there should be in any one of you an evil, unbelieving heart, in falling away from the living God. But encourage one another day after day, as long as it is still called 'Today,' lest any one of you be hardened by the deceitfulness of sin."*

1. Take an exacting look at your own life. In what area could you encourage your husband and soften your own heart at the same time?

2. Choose two things to do this week in the love language of your husband.

The statement that God is in control is either true or it's not true. If it's not true, we'd better forget about God. But if it is true, and we accept God's revelation of himself, our faith enables us to enjoy and rest in the certainty of his providence.

PAUL LITTLE

God Is Greater

The bravest thing I've ever done is parasailing. In case you're unfamiliar with the sport, this is how it works: First you're harnessed into an open parachute, and you're dragged screaming off a beach until you're high in the air. Then, young, teenage boys pull you around a bay in huge arcs behind a speedboat.

Just when you finally get brave enough to open your eyes, you notice that you're rushing like a misguided pigeon toward the eighth floor of your hotel. The young boys yell at you in some other language that you can barely hear, but this gets your attention — because you can now see your reflection in the hotel windows.

You realize, then, that the boys are motioning for you to pull on one side of the harness — the way they taught you when you were still on the ground. One of them keeps yelling, "Mas! Mucho mas!" That's Spanish for "Pull harder or you'll crash."

Of course I didn't crash. I landed safely. But later it amazed me to think how much trust I put in those teenage boys and that simple harness. Should I have? And for what? A thrill?

At times, trusting God with our husbands as they undergo spiritual change can feel almost as scary. Is God really greater than whatever situation we face with the men we chose to marry?

Joy enjoyed all the benefits that came from her husband's good job in advertising. Joy and Chris thrived on their busy but focused lifestyle. They bought a beautiful home in the suburbs of Chicago with cottonwood trees in the backyard. Two new cars sat in the garage, and two touring bikes graced the porch. Eventually, two children were born — a girl for Joy and a boy for Chris.

During this prosperous time, Chris and Joy got involved in a growing church and committed to a small group that met every other week in their living room. The group just happened to be grappling with purpose-in-life issues when Chris lost his job.

Chris sent résumés all over the country, but he couldn't shake the thoughts that crossed his mind during the group discussions. As he considered the direction of his life, he felt a change of focus was in order. In the end, he decided he wanted to join a small, non-profit organization in San Diego.

"It meant downscaling immensely," Joy said, "from a brand-new house in the suburbs of Chicago to a tiny little apartment."

Joy wrestled with the decision to move away from family, friends, their church, and the Bible study that were so important in their lives, and with the inevitable change in standard of living. "All the while I could just hear the Lord saying, 'How much do you trust Me in this one? Are you going to support Chris if this is really where I'm leading him to go?'"

Today, the word "trust" creates a paradox of feelings. It's something we want to practice, but it also hits us like an easy religious cliché. Too often those who offer advice, preach, or try to comfort whip out "trust" as a godly cure-all. Even when the Holy Spirit whispers it in our ears, it seems like the hardest thing to do. Half the time we aren't even sure what it looks like. Do we let go? Do we confront? Do we speak? Do we shut up?

Change in our lives, especially as it takes place in our husbands, flips trust out of the cliché realm and into the hard-to-live one. No longer does tomorrow feel comfortable — we don't know what to expect. The man we share our life with is in the throes of emotional and spiritual changes. He, more than likely, will recast the future of the family in some way. Maybe now he wants a ministry, or maybe now he's home a lot more. You're glad, but then again, how do you cope when you can no longer see familiar ground beneath you?

When you think about it, trust isn't just a religious issue. It's also a life issue. Unless you're in a padded room, curled up in a fetal position with total paranoia, trust is part of your life. We're all rushing toward a hotel window of some kind, ready to crash if we become too distracted by the threat itself. So when our husbands begin to change, the question is not *whether* we're trusting, but *what* we're trusting.

Where Trust Belongs

Joy's Bible study helped put the family's move from Chicago into perspective for her. Talking things through, she recognized that it was not so much Chris she needed to trust, but God himself. He'd take care of them. He'd provided in the past; He could provide everything she'd need in the future. "OK, honey," she told Chris. "We're off to San Diego."

Your husband may not be asking you to trust him by moving. Maybe he wants you to trust his promise that he loves you. Or maybe he's asking what seems like the impossible — for you to trust him to be faithful in the wake of infidelity. Maybe your doubts are rooted in irritating little husband-habits, or maybe in a crisis as big as bankruptcy.

Trust in a changing relationship has an interesting dynamic. On the one hand, trust is central to a healthy marriage. Trust is what provides security, often despite circumstances. It makes change easier because it brings with it a rock-solid base from which to grow. If trust exists between a husband and wife, neither will worry that the other will give up on him in the midst of change.

But human beings, full of foibles and failings and frustrations, will never be perfectly trustworthy. Try as I might, I could not find a Bible verse that said "trust in your husband." There were plenty of verses for respect, which has an element of trust in it. What my search pointed out to me is that trust, defined by my dictionary as "assured reliance on another's integrity, assured anticipation, confidence, hope," is best placed in God. He's the only One who's perfectly trustworthy.

The difficult thing about the future is just that — it's the future, and we don't know what it holds. The answer: Trust God, whom we can't physically see, touch, smell, taste, or hear. The reality: Live with a man whom we *can* see, whose five-o'clock shadow we can touch, whose breath smells like onions, whose excuses ring false in our ears. Love may be blind, but trust isn't. How can it bridge the gap between the answer and reality?

Trusting the Man in the Middle

Ron has gotten into gardening. One of his office windows looks immediately out onto a bank that he's planted with colorful flowers. No one else can see them, but they're important to him. He's spending more and more time out in the yard, putzing around. Ron's an orderly guy. He likes things neat and trimmed and under control. I do, too, within reason.

Once there was a sweet little tree that grew right outside our daughter's window. I asked Ron one day to shape up its straggly limbs while I went to the store. When I returned, there was one stalk left in the ground — no branches, no twigs, no leaves, no future. We had to pull it out.

One day last year he was out in our backyard and decided to trim back the bougainvillea. The full, creeping, bushy, brilliant, deep pink bougain-villea. Several hours later there was once again one stalk left in the ground. The view of the chain-link fence was now unobstructed. Whoopee. The bougainvillea's finally growing back, after a year.

I was standing at the sink doing dishes not long ago. Ron was pruning one of our three new, silver-dollar eucalyptus trees. His ladder tottered between the tree and the descending slope behind him. One minute he was there; the next minute he, the ladder, and the tree had disappeared over the edge of the slope. Now we have two silver-dollar eucalyptus trees.

Do I trust Ron with pruning shears? Should I?

Trust is a two-pronged proposition when it comes to our husbands. Trusting another person first requires a look at intentions, and second at actions. It's possible to trust someone's intention — his desire to change, his motivation, his attitude, his heart — while reserving approval for his actions until time has proven him trustworthy.

In some instances, broken trust is as easily regained as it was lost. In other cases, it may be years before total trust is restored. It depends upon the weight of the matter in the eyes of the one who was hurt.

Take Ron's pruning, which is not a big deal. Frankly, I don't trust Ron with the pruning shears. I may never. But I trust his heart and his motives regarding pruning. He's not trying to kill the trees. I trust, which means I *know*, that his goal is not to aggravate me but to tidy things up. I'm sure about it. Trust is being sure about something or someone.

As our husbands grow and change, our goal is to trust their hearts and respect their efforts. Most assuredly, they, like us, will fail or botch things up at times, maybe even on an enormous scale. But it is one thing to accept and expect imperfection; it's another to expect failure.

Mike swept Jennifer off her feet in high school. He was the quarterback on the football team, handsome, gregarious, fun to be around. When he asked her to marry him at eighteen, she thought his history with other women was over. They were caught up in each other and in what they thought marriage would be. But in three years, Mike had three affairs. When Jennifer found out, she was devastated, but not shocked. From the earliest days of their marriage, she'd felt sure she couldn't trust him with women.

Mike and Jennifer were both Christians, both young in age, experience, and faith, and both insecure. They didn't want to end their marriage, but there was a huge amount of work to save it. Mike took full responsibility for his wrongdoing, but as they talked through their three years together, he admitted that he had never really trusted himself — and perhaps Jennifer's constant lack of trust had played a big part in it. If the woman who loved him and knew him best thought he could be unfaithful, maybe she was right.

After some experienced counsel and deep soul-searching, Jennifer accepted her part in the troubled relationship. God continued His work in their tottering marriage. When Mike really turned the corner and apologized to Jennifer, convincing her that his heart's desire was to be the husband she wanted and needed, Jennifer did the hardest thing she had ever done in her life — she decided to trust him again. She couldn't trust his actions for a long, long time. He'd lost that privilege, and he had a long way to go to get to the point where she could. But she could trust his heart and expect it to succeed. When she made that choice, his defenses broke down, and he was eager to change.

When we expect our husbands to fail, when we demonstrate with our actions or words that they won't live up to some standard, more often than not those expectations are realized. If we don't trust them and make way for the changes they're working on, we take away their hope for the future, and we ignore the hope we could have for ours.

Trusting a man's heart and expecting success is risky. We risk pain, changed circumstances, and most of all, the security of control. Sometimes the risk may seem too high. So how can we do it?

Trusting our husbands, in the midst of change, in the midst of pain, has got to be a by-product of our trust in God.

Matters of Trust

Charlene's husband, Keith, used a credit card the way kids use a Nintendo joystick. Everything from breakfasts to a bench press showed up on their multipage bills. Charlene felt so much stress because of creditors and past-due accounts, she took matters into her own hands. She returned items, cut up credit cards when she could, and kept the money she earned from her job in her own account. Needless to say, fighting became a way of life for the two.

When Keith renewed his commitment to Christ, he was convicted about his spending habits. He cut back, some days doing better than others. He recognized Charlene handled money better than he did but felt they needed to start making financial decisions together. Charlene noticed Keith's changes but didn't trust them. It had taken three years just to get to the semicomfortable place she was. The thought of possibly falling back in the clutches of bill collectors scared her. She only felt secure when she was in control.

Eventually Keith became discouraged. Today they are divorced.

Charlene loves God and continues to seek to live for Him, but when it came to Keith's spending habits, somehow God was not as real as her circumstances. If we're honest, we'll admit Charlene is not alone. As much as we know we should trust God with every situation, we can't push some internal button and make it so.

We know God is perfect, in control, and He loves us, but it's hard to live this knowledge out. God is the beginning and the end, but we're in the middle with our husbands. How can He become real enough for us to trust Him with our lives? Here are some principles that have helped me stay harnessed by trust.

Little Things Are Little Things

I've been a mother for twenty years. In that time I've had periods of total control over two lives. When our children were little, I could recognize every stitch of clothing they owned. I knew every word of their vocabulary and when they first said it. I knew every bit of food that went in my kids' mouths and when it came out the other end as well. I was in charge of bedtime, waking-up time, nap time, playtime, TV time, and time-outs. As my children grew up, I had to let go, but it wasn't in one big lump. It was little by little.

When Suzanne had her daughter, she struggled to let her husband, Phil, take care of the baby. He was clumsy and didn't know what do to when she cried. More and more Suzanne found herself taking their little girl out of Phil's arms and caring for her.

Changing a diaper hardly qualified as the problem of the year, but it was the very place Suzanne needed to let go. Finally one day she called up a friend and said, "Can I come over for a couple of hours?" And she left the baby with Phil.

Though a small thing, Suzanne fretted all the way to her friend's house. "What if the baby cries the whole time I'm gone," she thought. "Oh Lord, help Phil know what to do." Over and over worries followed by prayers whittled away the two hours. When she got home, the baby was sound asleep, and her husband was reading the paper.

That day Suzanne built up her trust in God. She had let go, and God had taken care of her new baby and inexperienced husband.

Use small opportunities, as well as large ones, to learn how to trust.

Patience and Trust Are Close Friends

Trusting God's plan is inextricably bound up in having to wait for God's timing. In Psalm 37 we are instructed to "trust in the Lord" (vv. 3, 5) and then to "wait patiently for Him" (vs. 7).

Robert Hicks put it this way:

> The question I frequently hear is, "Why is it taking me so long to get better?" If spiritual life is viewed as life-changing events and commitments, there will be much disappointment and perhaps doubt about whether God is doing anything at all. But once the concept of journey is grasped, the expectations change. Each person's journey is different.... Once we embrace the journey concept, all the other aspects of spiritual

life can be understood in relationship to it.... Men need to be encour-
aged that no matter where they are on their spiritual journey, they
aren't home yet. They are still en route.[1]

John grew up in a family where he never learned what it meant to suf-
fer the consequences for his actions. He chose Giselle to be his wife in part
because she was an unaware but willing accomplice to John's irresponsibility.
She was eager to pick up the pieces he dropped. In a very real sense, John
went from one mother to another when he married Giselle.

When John joined a small Christian men's group, he observed models
of healthy Christian manhood. A year later he went to Promise Keepers,
where he was hit with two profound revelations — many men understood
just what he was feeling, and there was no more room for excuses about irre-
sponsible behavior.

John now has two other men in his life who hold him accountable. All
struggles are not over, however. John's changes are incremental, not giant,
steps. He slips; he moves ahead; he slips again. After watching her husband's
efforts, Giselle also is learning — to wait, not to nag or prod, and ultimately
to trust her husband and God.

Have you ever explored tide pools on an ocean beach? If so, then you've
undoubtedly seen a sea anemone, the soft, tentacled, round creature that
fixes itself to a rock. When you poke at sea anemones, they close. You can
actually poke and poke a sea anemone to death.

I wonder if, in the same way, we can kill the spirit of change we see our
husbands embracing. When we poke at our husbands, their spirits close.
When we badger them to become what we're waiting for, we're in danger of
closing them so tightly they may never open up again.

Even God Can't Be "Trusted"

One of the reasons it's hard to trust God is because He isn't always what we
want Him to be. He lets us feel pain. He lets consequences teach us about

sin. He answers our godly prayers sometimes by saying no.

Kathy's husband, Bill, was an avid fisherman. He tied his own flies, built his own rods, and headed for a river or lake every Saturday possible. At first Kathy went along, but when babies arrived, keeping track of toddlers by rushing water proved more than she could handle. As a result Kathy spent more and more Saturdays taking care of kids and doing yard work. That's when the fighting began.

Kathy prayed for Bill to change, but month after month she found herself spending weekends alone. One day after a particularly bad blowup, Kathy seethed as she pushed the lawnmower. The Holy Spirit's calming whispers kept invading her rush of angry thoughts. She shoved them aside and thought, "If I listen to You, I'll mow the lawn for the rest of my life."

Immediately a whispered thought came. "You have to give Me that option."

To trust God, we need to give up what we want Him to be, relinquish our own agendas, and let God intervene with our husbands where we can't.

Trust Is Farsighted

Perspective is a key concept for me, particularly during change. I must remind myself that I'm promised an eternity in heaven and that my life on earth by comparison is a mere moment in time. The daily stuff I deal with as my husband changes doesn't feel quite so weighty when compared with eternity.

I once heard Pastor Charles Stanley talking about perspective in relation to pain of any kind. He said, roughly, that when we've been in heaven a hundred years we'll look back at earth and remark at how tough those painful years were. When we've been in heaven a thousand years, we'll look back at earth and barely remember our visit there. Then when we've been in heaven ten thousand years, we won't even care. That's what I'm looking forward to — eternity in a place with no pain or tears or worries or end.

A young mother, whose every day with three preschoolers feels like an eternity, told me about her husband's new faith. "I'm frustrated right now because being a Christian doesn't mean he'll automatically be a better person," she said. "But it means where there once was no hope, there is now hope."

Even though she could tell me specific ways her husband was changing, she was feeling hopeless and alone at that moment, overwhelmed with the kinds of burdens all mothers of young children carry at times. I remember so well spending whole days doing nothing measurable. Some days Ron would come home to a family room sprinkled like a cupcake with every conceivable toy and all its pieces, and no dinner. I remember thinking my life would never change, my children would never grow up, my husband would never understand.

But those were the times I learned to force myself to see the bigger picture — to look ahead like a scout to the future I knew would come, to look back at the past to see how things had changed, and to look at how we all had grown. In time my life did change. My children did grow. My husband did, and does, understand most of the time.

Perspective is a word to hold before you when you wonder if you can stand it one more day. It gives you hope. And with hope we can stand a lot of change. When my perspective is farsighted, my eyes are on God, and my hope is in God. When my eyes are on myself or my circumstances, so is my hope. And that's no hope at all.

Praying Is Believing

Prayer is one thing we can do to influence our husbands without meddling at all. As a result, it is an incredible trust builder. Watching God work when we've consciously talked over the situation with Him, makes Him so "see-able," so touchable — so real.

I remember the day my mother's possible death from cancer hit me. I was walking the track behind my house and praying. For a while all I could say was "Heal her, heal her, heal her." Over and over I poured out my heart — no complete sentences, probably no complete thoughts. I badgered God with my feelings and my wishes and hopes. I told Him without mincing any words exactly what I wanted and when I wanted it. Philippians 4:6 gives me the right to tell Him *everything* on my heart. I didn't demand He answer the way I wished, but I didn't hold back from saying what I wanted to say either.

God is like that — He allows us to pester Him. He wants it. He is so available, anytime, anywhere, regardless of the condition of our emotions or thoughts. All He asks is that we deal with our own sin first so there is no wall between His perfection and our imperfection. I don't have any problem with that. "My sins are ever before me," said David. I feel exactly the same way. My sins are ever before me, so I get them out of the way first when I go to talk to the Lord. It's a pleasure to get them off my back.

By the way, my mother died. I was forty-one — too young to lose a mother. We always are. God didn't do everything I asked, but somehow I knew He was there, working things out beyond my loss and heartache. I felt comfort at the same time I felt pain.

Godly trust is a paradox. Whether you're confronting trust as an easy-spoken cliché and a hard-lived reality, or experiencing its peace in pain, it cannot be summed up or pinned down in fifteen pages or one hundred pages! To grasp it, it must be lived. And what better time to live it than when our husbands are trying to make new promises. Sometimes the buildings look a little close, the changing scenery can be dizzying, and courage is hard to find. I just hope I'm brave enough to live with open eyes and a full chute, choosing to trust God with the one He gave me to love.

Promising Conversations

Jeremiah 29:11 — "'For I know the plans that I have for you,' declares the LORD, 'plans for welfare and not for calamity to give you a future and a hope.'"

Proverbs 3:5–6 — "Trust in the LORD with all your heart, and do not lean on your own understanding. In all your ways acknowledge Him, and He will make your paths straight."

Romans 15:13 — "May the God of hope fill you with all joy and peace as you trust in him, so that you may overflow with hope by the power of the Holy Spirit" (NIV).

James 1:2–4 — "Consider it all joy, my brethren, when you encounter various trials; knowing that the testing of your faith produces endurance. And let endurance have its perfect result, that you may be perfect and complete, lacking in nothing."

1. Trust is central to a healthy marriage. In what areas do you find it easy to trust your husband?

2. If trust has been broken, where and how do you begin to rebuild it?

3. Even when you can't trust in man, you can trust in God. How do trials and temptations strengthen your faith? What examples can you think of in your own life?

Private Considerations

Romans 12:12 — *"rejoicing in hope, persevering in tribulation, devoted to prayer."*

1. Truthfully, honestly, do you place more trust in God's plan or in your husband's actions? Do you need to make any adjustments?

2. Memorize and meditate on the three commands of Romans 12:12. Then take at least fifteen minutes to write to the Lord — a letter, a journal-like page, a psalm. Use this time to reflect on God and your husband and to measure what are realistic expectations of each. Come to the place where you are willing to accept the God who is, not the God you want.

Friends are like trees. There is refuge beneath their branches. There is safety. There is a haven to come to, no matter what. No matter the time (day or night), the weather (fair or foul), or the circumstances (pleasant or painful), trees and friends stay steady, strong, and faithful. Like a deep-rooted oak, friends weather the storms, hang on through the droughts, and grow stronger through the years.

STU WEBER

Friends Need Friends

I believe John and I are still married because of the prayers and commitment of a few close friends," Giselle said. "When John decided to ask two men to check on his growth as a husband, to hold his feet to the fire, our marriage really began to change. His accountability to a few buddies took enormous pressure off our relationship."

Over the years John had let Giselle handle the family decisions. Even paying the bills became easy to avoid. When he finally accepted the job again, the struggle wasn't over. But this time John made himself answerable to two friends. John admitted, "They gave me the incentive I needed. I knew I'd see them on Tuesday night, and I didn't want to face them unless I'd followed through on at least some of their suggestions."

John's friends helped him regain his sense of responsibility and competence as a husband and father.

We've talked about change and growth in our husbands — what's happening and why and how to discover our roles in it. We've also seen pictures of men who've made incredible steps to break out of harmful patterns of behavior, and the women in their lives who've helped clear the way.

What part do friends have in our husbands' changes? And in ours? How can we encourage those relationships?

Making friends is not so hard for us wives. Our children pave the way many times. And for some reason, we women have known for a long time that we need to connect with other women to help us through "wife-ing," child raising, and the other demands on our lives. We've seen that feedback from knowledgeable sources is invaluable, especially during times of significant change.

Today many men are making the same discovery. In the midst of their demanding work schedules, they're reacting against the sad commentary on friendship expressed by Patrick Morley in *The Man in the Mirror*. "I think most men could recruit six pallbearers," he says, "but hardly anyone has a friend he can call at 2:00 A.M."

Men are now finding that friends can be helpful change-makers. They're using their former teammates as sounding boards and catalysts and are opening themselves up to intimate male friendships — sometimes for the first time.

Not surprisingly, some wives find it hard to accept that their husbands need close male friends. They're wary that this new camaraderie might interfere with the intimacy they have with their husbands. "Why can't I be that friend for my husband?" they ask.

Tim Kimmel answered that question for us in chapter three when he said, "We're talking about a different type of love, meeting a different need." It's not possible for one human being to meet all the needs of another.

Life is a battle we can fight alone or with comrades. We can choose to share our burdens or get buried under them. "Where there is no guidance, the people fall," says Solomon in Proverbs 11:14. "But in abundance of counselors there is victory."

Friends on Every Level

There are many levels of friendships, just as there are many levels of communication — from nodding acquaintances to bosom buddies to mentors. As wives of changing men, who are relating in ways we've never seen before, the more we acknowledge the different levels of friendship men need, the less we'll feel threatened.

Ron plays tennis every Saturday morning he's in town at a court frequented by dozens of men from our community. Often he'll play with the same guys, if they show up, though they're not confirmed partners. These guys are acquaintances, like the people you nod at in the grocery store.

Once in a blue moon, one of these men will call to set something up. That's another level — exchanged phone numbers, names, and occupations.

Then there's "I'm playing tennis with David Tuesday afternoon." Now Ron's scheduling a time to do something he likes with someone he particularly likes to do it with.

And when he and David sit in the Jacuzzi after the game for an hour, talking about business and their wives and children, the level of relating has taken a giant step toward intimacy.

Ron has worked hard over the past several years to build up his friendships. He now has a bunch of guys who perform different, significant roles in his life. Because of his independent nature, it's a struggle, but he's determined to become more confidential and open with several other men.

"When I meet with my group of men every week," Ron says in *Make a Life, Not Just a Living,* "we ask one another hard questions — potentially embarrassing questions — such as:

- Did you consistently give your employer an honest day's work?
- Did you do anything this week that could hurt your reputation?
- Were you in any compromising situation with someone of the opposite sex?
- Did you spend quality time with your children?

• Was your integrity impeccable?"

And the last question his accountable friends ask him? "Have you lied to me?"

Ron goes on to say, "If you're serious about developing positive qualities in your life, you will need to say to a few others, 'I want you to hold me accountable. You have access to my life, and if you ever see anything in me that needs to change, tell me. You're my friend, and I know you want the best for me.'"[1]

This is the accountability men are looking for and wives know their husbands need.

Hal's given two guys the freedom to confront him on any area of his life. With these men he is very open and vulnerable and honest. They don't let him get away with anything. His wife doesn't know what they talk and pray about — it's confidential. But she trusts Hal to use these men to help him grow and to keep him committed to her. It's for his own good. And hers, too.

Accountability is reserved for friends whose hearts connect on a spiritual level. When our husbands know their best buddies are tackling issues with the Bible in one hand and empathy in the other, they are ready to face the tough issues and ask and answer the revealing questions.

For instance, "Johnny was caught with speed at school last week. Please pray for me. I'm so frustrated with his attitude I want to punch him!" Or, "A gorgeous secretary in our office came on to me yesterday. I can't stop thinking about her. What do I do?"

Accountability is rarely a one-sided experience. One of the exciting things about this kind of relationship is what it can do for all involved. When one person is open and vulnerable, it encourages others to be the same. We learn from others close to us, and when we see growth from the bottom up, along with all the adjustment and change, it teaches us ways to deal with our own lives.

The following word picture from *As Iron Sharpens Iron* by Howard and

Bill Hendricks (father and son) is a masterful illustration of what committed friends can mean in our lives, whether we're men or women:

> *Too many men are trying to go it alone in terms of their marriage and family life, their personal life, their work, or their spiritual commitments. They are trying to scale mountains of Himalayan proportions on the strength of rugged independence.*
>
> *It won't work. Men need mentors, seasoned guides to help them along the way. Bob Biehl of Masterplanning Group International has pointed out that mentoring is like a group of men scaling a mountain. If a guy is linked to another guy above him, and that man in turn is linked to other men farther up the cliff, then together they have safety, stability, and strength. If a man slips and begins to fall, fifteen or twenty climbers absorb the impact and pull him back from disaster.*
>
> *But imagine a man climbing alone, with no support system. He may achieve great heights. But one wrong move and he can fall thousands of feet to his death, without so much as anyone hearing his cry. That's why Scripture says, "Two are better than one because they have a good return for their labor. For if either of them falls, the one will lift up his companion. But woe to the one who falls when there is not another to lift him up" (Ecclesiastes 4:9–10).[2]*

"Mentor" is another word and concept that's resurfacing these days as more people acknowledge the expertise that comes with age and the need we all have to connect with those wiser than we are.

"Mentoring is all about people development," say Howard and Bill Hendricks. They've devoted their entire book to the concept. In it they encourage each of us to find a Paul (a mentor), a Barnabas (a good friend), and a Timothy (what they call a protégé, someone who learns from us). Regardless of our ages, we can find these three types of relationships if we pray and look for them.

That's successful Christian living: learning from a master, sharing with a peer, training someone "younger" (not necessarily in age, but possibly in knowledge and understanding).

It would be wonderful to take three mice, wave a magic wand, and turn them into a small group, or a Paul, Barnabas, and Timothy, for our husbands. While it's really up to them to recognize their need, there are things we can do to encourage these relationships:

- Be willing to reach out to wives of men your husband wants to get to know. Don't limit your social interactions to your friends alone. While this may be more comfortable for you, it doesn't empower your husband to make friends of *his* choice.
- Make it possible for him to schedule time with his men friends. Let him take Saturday mornings for tennis; get dinner on the table early or late enough to give him time for friend-building; loosen up the family's plans so all his free time is not filled.
- Revive the vanishing art of hospitality. Invite couples, or families, over for dinner and/or games to nurture relationships.
- If he's willing, help him think through the men he knows. Ask him if any of these friends share his values and commitment to growth. He may even find a soul mate in a man whose children are the same ages as yours. Together these men could grow in several areas — and take their kids along with them.
- Encourage his participation at men's retreats. Does this mean saving money? Marking the calendar? Planning a trip to your mother's on that weekend?

Your Own Friends of Change

Having our own accountable relationships, especially during times when our husbands are changing, can be just as important to us as it is to them. Remember Elizabeth and Jimmy from chapter seven? It was years before

Elizabeth could muster up the courage, or release the frustration, to tell someone the struggles she was having with Jimmy's drinking. She called me late one evening and asked if we could have coffee.

When her story and her tears flowed out of her hurting heart, I didn't know what to say. She faced a debilitating situation I knew nothing about. I'm not a counselor. I didn't know what I had to offer except love and compassion. But our conversation was the beginning of an accountable relationship and the beginning of change. Elizabeth and I talk frequently about her marriage and her response to Jimmy. And she has two other close friends who help her evaluate her behavior. She's honest with us and lets us help her keep true to her convictions, which in her case means following through on some difficult tough-love measures, while allowing God to work changes in her own life.

When Jimmy saw Elizabeth's determination to work on their marriage, as well as to make the changes she needed, he also talked to a friend and asked him to hold him accountable. From that, came wonderful counseling with a professional who knew what to do in this difficult situation. And in time, growth and health and healing came.

Our friends can be a support, like Joshua was for Moses, to "hold up our arms" in the midst of battle.

That's what Giselle feels as she and John work at growing together. "I have my friends to dump stuff on, instead of John," she told me. "And John has his buddies. They're not telling us what we *want* to hear but what we *need* to hear. We're still together because we've had to answer to those friends."

I find that even with the many good friends I have, I don't give away the privilege of accountability too easily. I can only handle being answerable to a few. Taking our intimacy to that deep level with too many women is wearing (because they're being transparent as well) and could be threatening to your situation. Just imagine keeping tabs on the sticky points of a difficult situation, after confiding in twenty-five people!

It takes time and prayer to find the right combination of wisdom and candor, personality and spirituality in an accountable friend or small group. To others you can say, "I don't get along with Jerry's mother, but her birthday is next week, and she's coming for three days. Please pray for me, and call me Saturday morning to see if I've been faithful to be kind to her."

Say you've found two other friends who've agreed to this mutual discipleship. For that's what it is — discipling one another to be like Jesus. What do you do when you're together? Is there a set plan? How often do you meet?

There is no set way of forming an accountability group, but here are things to keep in mind.

- Small groups work best. No more than a few. Maybe your "group" is only you and a friend.
- Commitment makes a difference. You might want to set a trial period for several weeks. But when you decide to commit, do it. This isn't like a casual discussion group where people flow in and out.
- Meeting frequently matters. Decide your own schedule, but if you let too much time pass between meetings, you'll spend your time catching up and reestablishing your openness. Your accountability friends may not even live in the same city as you do. However, if you're dealing with a particularly difficult issue, you may want an accountability friend who lives near you. Somehow face-to-face connection provides stronger motivation.
- Shorter is better. Meet for a short enough time that you won't be tempted to skip if your schedule fills up.
- Complete confidentiality is necessary for complete honesty.
- Choose your timing and your words carefully. Often women are more sensitive to advice than men. It's not easy for us to hear criticism or to be frank and open, even if it's true and timely. Gentleness must go hand in hand with honesty.
- A group is to help you grow, not to gossip.

- Openness breeds openness. It is very healing to be able to share openly with someone who pledges to understand, to pray, to reserve judgment, and to be vulnerable herself. But sometimes you have to be the one to start.

And therein is wisdom. We have one life, and most likely one marriage, here on earth. We can fly carelessly through it — like a golf ball from my driver — without an ounce of thoughtful placement. Or we can be a golf ball in the hands of a master, skillfully going just where it should. Friends, mentors, accountability relationships can have a lot to do with the excellence of our lives. They can keep us on the right fairways, help us out of sand traps, and give us a chance to help them, too.

When I was on vacation, I ran into a friend, who started crying as soon as she saw me. She cried so hard I couldn't imagine what was wrong. Back in her room she poured out her heart to me and confessed to an adulterous relationship she was ending. My shoulder and my compassion were all she needed then.

I've kept her confidence, sometimes sharing the situation but never the identity, even with Ron. We've been able to confide on a deep level. I ask her frankly how she's coping, and she asks me to pray when she knows she'll run into this man again. I'm not wiser or older or more experienced. I'm just her friend. We're in it together.

Being "in it together" is the twine that binds friends. The "it" isn't necessarily a specific location or situation — it's just life. What's going on in my life may not be exactly what's going on in yours. But we're all dealing with similar struggles: How do I "work out my salvation"? How can I defer to my husband when he doesn't defer to me? What kind of limits should I set for my teenager? What does it mean to be "in the world but not of it"?

Our peers, at least those with whom we spend the choicest time, have a huge influence on our attitudes, our actions, and our convictions. As parents, we spend a lot of time discussing our children's peer groups. But good peer groups are just as important for us. When we link ourselves together like people climbing the same mountain at the same time (even when some are farther ahead or behind), we have a sense of teamwork. We're there for one another, committed to the same quest. Our ropes are tested and strong, and if we slip, we know they'll hold. And our friends will be there, hanging on.

Our families are constantly going through changes — internal and external. And with the help of our friends, we can all be the stronger for it. If we hold on to our husbands too tightly, or if we ignore our own need for outside support, we could lose more than we think. We'll be taking away some of those other mountain climbers whose ropes could be securely fastened to our husbands' waists, and to ours.

After all, we're partners in promise, with our husbands and our friends. We've chosen to share our lives with one another and to become the women and men God wants us to be. Is there any reason not to hook up with friends who can help us grow?

Promising Conversations

Proverbs 27:17 — *"Iron sharpens iron, so one man sharpens another."*

Proverbs 18:24b — *"There is a friend who sticks closer than a brother."*

Proverbs 27:6a — *"Faithful are the wounds of a friend."*

1. How do you feel about your husband finding and confiding in a group of men?

2. Do you ever find yourself hindering your husband's friendships? How?

3. What can you do about it, or how can you encourage his friendships?

4. How would you say strong friendships are built?

5. Do you have a group that is supporting you? What do you look for in friends?

Private Considerations

1. Can you think of any men your husband might relate well to in a Paul (mentor), a Barnabas (buddy), or a Timothy (protégé) relationship? List their names, and begin to pray to that end.

2. Can you think of any women that might be Paul, Barnabas, or Timothy relationships for you? List them and pray.

3. The best accountability is a prayer partner. Identify one or several women who might be this kind of friend to you. Pray about asking her.

Even if I were some kind of Superwoman (and I am not), I would still only be able to supply [my children] with the wealth of the feminine, wondrous though it is. It takes a man — preferably their father — to provide the deep masculine input that rounds out their world and opens up the mysteries of adulthood. Children need their fathers.

NANCY SWIHART

Partners in Parenting

Parenting is scary now," Ted says, thinking about his boys, who are five and eight. He wasn't worried about parenting at first, he explains. And he had no trouble falling in love with his boys. "But balancing all the competing demands is a lot more difficult than I thought it would be."

One night while watching his oldest boy sleep, Ted felt overwhelmed by the realization that he wasn't living up to the standard he'd set for himself. As he later prayed and cried in his own bed, God gave him a new perspective on fathering.

"You know when you look into a series of mirrors and it telescopes the image away from you, smaller and smaller?" Ted asks. "It seems your image could go on forever. That's the way it is with your kids. If my business collapsed today, my customers would be upset for a couple of weeks, or until they found another provider. They wouldn't even remember me after a while. But when you love your kids, the impact goes on and on and on.

There's an eternal quality about that love, making it more important than any other investment."

Many men are beginning to see what Ted is learning. There's an ongoing return when the family is a top priority. If a dad loves his kids, they'll love their kids, who'll love their kids. "It's not that earning a living isn't important," Ted concluded. "It just doesn't have that recurring return, year after year, generation after generation."

A big result of the men's movement is a family revival. Men are reordering their priorities, refocusing their energies, reworking their goals, and rediscovering their kids. Many of them have begun to understand the huge impact they have on their children, and they're readjusting their lives to show it.

However, making changes in the family is harder than it looks. What really happens when dad comes home from work at night and five-year-old Johnny begs him to play outside? How much of the inspiration men feel at meetings translates into action at home? And how can wives be partners in the promise of family growth?

Women often feel overwhelmed by the task of mothering. But just as often, and maybe more so, our husbands feel perplexed about fathering. Being a dad is in some ways tougher today than in the past. Time together isn't built into the schedule as when dads took their children to the barn or the fields to work with them. Families in general are separated, too busy, too distracted, too bombarded by the media, too imploded by pressure.

As a result, men are insecure in their relationships with their children. It's scary to face the reality that others are counting on you — on your judgment, on your choices, on your strength, on your values.

Could this help explain the following statistics from *Today's Father?* The magazine, a publication of the National Center for Fathering, reported on a survey of 1621 men from six different Promise Keepers' rallies in 1994. Their representation was mixed racially, economically, and denominationally, but did reflect Promise Keepers' largely white and Protestant attendees. Of those surveyed, 68.3 percent were satisfied with their marriages, 71.5 percent felt satisfied with their wife as a spouse — and yet only 25 percent indicated satisfaction with themselves as fathers.

Though this last low percentage is discouraging in one way, it's positive in another. We work on areas we aren't satisfied with. And the men's movement reflects that dissatisfaction and the desire to change. Listen to more statistics from *Today's Father*:

- The number of fathers receiving direct services from the National Center for Fathering has grown from five thousand fathers in 1993 to seventy-five thousand in 1995.

- The National Fatherhood Initiative is kicking off a national campaign to get community leaders talking about how to encourage responsible fatherhood.

- Several corporations are offering support or training specifically for fathers. (According to *Personnel Journal*, 60 percent of Fortune 500 companies offer parenting-education programs.)

- In 1987, a *Fortune* magazine poll found 30 percent of fathers said they had personally turned down a job promotion or transfer because it would have reduced the time they spend with their families.

- In a 1991 survey, 75 percent of the men said they would trade rapid career advancement for the chance to leave more time open to their families (*Dallas Morning News*).

- Vice-President Al Gore told four hundred civic leaders at the National Fatherhood Summit in Dallas in October 1994, "There can be nothing more noble than to see a father succeed."[1]

If your husband is going through spiritual renewal, God will begin working on his relationship with your children, but it won't be easy. Your encouragement of his efforts can make a big difference in his continuing to make changes — even small ones. As men press forward in their commitments, and wives continue to pray and partner with them, miracles are taking place.

Just ask Jimmy.

Jimmy's struggle with his alcoholism spilled over into his relationships with his children. Although he's always been an active father, his anger was unreasonable at times and created an undercurrent of instability. Recently I called Elizabeth to ask her what's been going on in her house now that her husband has made such a strong turn for the better.

"I can't believe you called just now!" she said with a laugh. "Jimmy and Alex are on a fishing trip in Alaska. This is the child who's so much like Jimmy and who Jimmy has the hardest time relating to. I'd been praying for God to do something in their relationship. Then this trip came up, and Jimmy actually wanted to take Alex. This is a huge step for him. In the past he would've gone alone, with his brother, or with our other son. Alex was so excited to be spending all this time alone with his dad."

It's taken a lot of bravery and hard work for Jimmy to get where he is now. But not all families are watching dads don their hero suits and burst out of phone booths ready to challenge the world on behalf of their wives and children. Some wives continue to experience conflict with their husbands in the realm of parenthood.

Ripples in the Stream

My friend's teenage kids love the out-of-doors. Often her daughter seeks a stream to sit by and soak in its tranquillity. Her sons also seek out streams — to plop worms in, or rocks, or whatever is handy. More than once their opposite ideas about stream use have come into direct conflict.

In the same way, husbands and wives often have different ideas about the shared task of parenthood. For example, it's hard to adjust to a husband's "rippling" effect on children's various activities. Inevitably we get the kids settled down for bed, and our husbands start roughhousing with them. We just get a baseball injury healed, and our husbands are out holding batting practice. Or we see the need for fatherly attention, and they see what's on TV.

Lucy's husband, Chad, is not a natural-born father. He has several grown children from his first marriage and two small boys in this one. He's had trouble in the past getting down to their level, literally and figuratively.

"When he comes home at night, he wants to see that the house is picked up," Lucy says. "He doesn't think to ask about, or even consider, the kids. But God's changing him little by little, in His timing. Chad's Bible study is forcing him to see more deeply into his own character," Lucy explains. "I can tell God's cracking that door open, but it's hard to picture it open wide."

When we married these guys, we had no idea of the many opportunities we'd have to learn, compromise, give up, accept, acquiesce, agree, and combine. Parenting is just one more opportunity for two to become one. Most dads feel the same commitment we do. So where do so many parenting conflicts come from?

The conflicts we experience in parenting, while not always erupting in all-out confrontations, are nevertheless challenging. Often they arise because we bring different gender styles, different histories, and different levels of learning into our parenting and our marriages.

She-Bears and He-Bears

It's often said that mothers are like protective she-bears; when their children are threatened, sometimes mothers react more out of instinct than reason. Ever since we felt that little guy or girl kicking around inside us, our protective "feelers" have sharpened in sensitivity. No wonder we tend to take on the protective role in parenting.

Recent research confirms that moms treat infants and toddlers, whether boys or girls, nearly the same, while dads play differently with their male and female children. They coo softly to the girls and wrestle with the boys. Dads tend to be less emotional and more objective in their parenting and are often better at follow-through. Most moms I know respond emotionally first.

While defining male and female roles is often helpful, it's important not to use the word "always." Most often couples consciously, or unconsciously, balance each other out. If a dad is protective, a mom is often more free to play other roles in parenting. If a dad takes risks with the kids, a mom might be more cautious. Trouble comes when roles become too rigid or when behaviors that might complement one another become points of conflict instead.

Many years ago, when Matt was about seven and Molly was four, Ron and I were on a business/ministry trip in Europe. We were gone for three weeks, during which time our kids stayed with their grandparents. One night in Germany I had this overwhelming desire to call home. I couldn't tell whether I was merely missing the kids or something was wrong. I told Ron I wanted to call that night. For some reason he didn't think we should. I don't remember whether it was money or inconvenience, but we had a big argument. The more we argued, the more frantic I got.

Ron didn't relent. I didn't either. So, around 4:00 A.M. I sneaked out of our room and went to the lobby to call Ron's parents. Everything was fine, and I was much relieved.

I was not so relieved, however, when I saw Ron coming down the stairs at 4:20 A.M. But now I was ready to deal with him. My kids were fine, and I was under control. Ron apologized profusely for not recognizing the depth of my mother-consciousness, and I apologized profusely for not being able to discuss the issue in a rational manner. He learned a lot that night about mothers and the enormous hold our children have over us.

While we both can point to instances where we disagreed with the other's approach, we've seen the outplaying of our different styles of parenting and the balance it's given our children. If Matt and Molly didn't have Ron, they'd be overprotected and underchallenged. If they didn't have me, they might be seriously injured.

As we balance our parenting approaches, Ron's in charge of the active stuff; I'm in charge of the aesthetics. He builds forts outside in the trees for the kids to spy from; I build them in the living room for story time. He's in charge of cars and bicycles; I'm in charge of seat belts and helmets. He kills rats; I kill ants. He baits the hooks; I read the books (even in the boat!).

The Pot Roast Factor

A story is told about a young woman who was preparing a roast for dinner. Her husband was with her in the kitchen, and he watched, puzzled, as she sliced off the end of the pot roast, which he considered the tastiest part, before she put it in the roasting pan.

"Why did you slice the end off the roast?" he asked.

"Well," she hesitated, "Mom always did."

"But why?" he pushed.

"I don't know," she admitted. "Let's call her and find out." So they did.

"Mom, why do you cut off the end of the roast before you cook it?"

"I don't know, honey. Grandma always did though. Why don't you call and ask her." So they did.

"Grandma, why do you cut off the end of the roast before you cook it?"

"Because my roaster's so small" came the answer.

How many things do we do in a certain way just because we saw it modeled?

Parenting and marriages are inextricably bound up in the parental relationships we had growing up. The trick comes in retaining and reusing the good stuff, and forgiving and forgetting the bad. For that reason I would urge you to look into those years of your life when your parents were your primary source of input.

Streams of Togetherness

In parenting theory, we know a lot of the right answers. We know moms need to let dads participate. We know we have weak areas that need someone's different strengths to fill. We know that things in our past which need correcting are better seen by another. So how do we blend our parenting differences into a stream of togetherness, rather than fight about them? How do we become a partner in this part of the promise?

Bridge the Information Gap

Parenting conflicts often arise for lack of information or understanding. An approach to discipline that seems second nature to us, but completely beyond our husbands, is probably the result of time and input we take for granted. I would bet that most women reading this book have taken advantage of some of the many sources of information on how to grow as a parent.

Think about all the opportunities you've had to learn.

Do you recognize these names: Dobson, Kimmel, Smalley, Rainey, Swindoll? I'll bet you're familiar with the teachings of at least one of them. Chances are, between your Bible study, your radio listening, your reading, and your discussions with friends, you're much higher on the "parental educational scale" than your husband.

As many books as my husband reads each year, I bet he's read very few on parenting since our children were born. Most husbands don't read even one. When I give Ron a book I'd like him to read, on any subject, he's more than happy to accept it from my hands, but he's not likely to read it with dispatch — unless I've dog-eared some pages or highlighted some points I want him to see.

Bite-sized chunks of information often work better for dads. They're more likely not to interrupt, intimidate, or inundate. If your husband is interested, there are several ways you can offer condensed information.

- Copy a chapter of a book that you think is particularly applicable. Then highlight the most important points, and give the chapter to him.
- Summarize an approach to an issue and type it out so he can read it.

- Transcribe a great tape you've heard, highlighting what you want him to "hear."

Before you take any of these steps, though, look over the lay of the land. Tim Kimmel told me his wife, Darcy, packed a copy of *What Wives Wish Their Husbands Knew about Women* in his suitcase one time. "I knew exactly what she wanted me to do — read this book!" But he was also quick to say, "Our relationship was at the point where it could handle something like that." Good reminder.

Become a Transitional Family

Partly due to the Christian men's movement, many Christian families are becoming transitional families as they examine what it means to live in light of the Bible. "Transition" means to pass from one thing to another. A transitional family can pass from ill health to good health, from dysfunction to full function. By becoming a transitional family, we impede or even halt the effect of our ancestors' indiscretions.

Exodus 34:6b–7 gives parents an incredible promise, along with a serious warning. "The LORD, the LORD God, compassionate and gracious, slow to anger, and abounding in lovingkindness and truth; who keeps lovingkindness for thousands, who forgives iniquity, transgression and sin, yet He will by no means leave *the guilty* unpunished, visiting the iniquity of fathers on the children and on the grandchildren to the third and fourth generations."

Generational sin needs to be addressed, and men turning to God desire to do so. However, by sin's very nature, it's hard to see in ourselves. A loving spouse can sometimes provide a voice of objectivity.

Beth is sixteen years younger than Mitch. She married him when she was just twenty, but after a while she saw what he couldn't. "When I realized Mitch was trying to live up to his father's standards, I finally had to get his attention," Beth said.

Having many responsibilities throughout his childhood produced a take-charge kind of guy. Mitch was used to giving orders and didn't know how to relate on an emotional level. He brought that behavior into his marriage and was ready to bestow it upon his children until Beth confronted him. "Don't you see," she said, "we're living our lives around what pleases your parents."

That was all it took to get Mitch to look more carefully at his fathering style. "Mitch is bent toward overworking our kids. But he's so aware of it now that he bends over backwards to avoid it. I've never seen a man so involved with his children on their level," Beth says.

It was Beth who asked Mitch to look at his fathering, but it was Mitch who broke the cycle. Mitch's parents, like many of ours, are from a generation that didn't talk openly about personal needs and shortcomings. Mitch doesn't blame them; he's learned from them, and he's honored them for all the good they did. This attitude frees him to make changes.

What can we do to take these men of ours and build up their fathering skills and commitment? We can't take over for them — although many women have had to do that for a time. Hopefully, their job as mom *and* dad will be cut in half as their husbands realize the joy that involved fathering brings. Following are some ideas for wives who want to encourage involved fathering — with this catch: Each suggestion should be done in a way that communicates respect.

Remind your husband of special occasions. One year, as is often the case, I did the Christmas shopping for our children and extended family without Ron. It didn't occur to me to apprise him of my purchases till Christmas morning when I saw the forlorn look on his face as he realized he couldn't share my excitement at the surprises. We had a talk, and I realized how much he hates to shop, and yet he still wants to be involved.

I'm also careful, but not always successful, to put the kids' schedules, vacations, and special occasions on his calendar. I still have to coach him to remember all our birthdays. Similarly, there are things Ron reminds me to do as well. The motivation is partnership, not pressure.

Make him part of your children's lives, even when it looks impossible. My friend Linda Weber thought up a brilliant scheme to keep Vietnam-bound Stu involved in their firstborn's life. Stu read on tape the children's books his boy had. Linda would hold Kent in her lap and turn the pages of the book, keeping time with Stu's reading. "No child of hers was going to lose touch with his father if she had anything to do with it. Even Uncle Sam couldn't interrupt story time," says Stu.

Just last week I used our video recorder to film Molly getting ready for her very first date because Ron was gone, and he didn't want to miss it.

Honor him in front of the kids. We made them together, but we often don't think alike when it comes to raising them. Still, we recognize the need to affirm our husbands' roles as fathers. Men need respect more than any other gift we can offer. When we honor our husbands in front of our children, we affirm the position and authority of fatherhood, we affirm the choice of husbands we made, we affirm the potential that is within these men, we affirm the security of our marriages and the families that all children, and husbands, long for.

Say things like...

"Wasn't your daddy great to teach you how to catch that grounder?"

"Isn't it nice to have Dad home tonight? It's so much more fun when we're all together."

"Molly, you need to look for a man just like your dad."

"Matt, I hope you're watching your dad to see how to treat your wife someday."

Offer helpful ideas for spending time together. I suspect that part of the mystique of fathering could be dispelled with a little help from us moms. Dads tend to think that playing with their children needs to be an all-day activity. Help him schedule a ten-minute batting practice or a twenty-minute card game. Dispel his fears about tea parties — they don't usually last long at all. Show him how to dance with his daughter as she stands on his shoes.

My dad used to play "Rain" with my son Matt. Dad would pull the covers off the bed, then he and Matt would settle down to an imaginary picnic — when all of a sudden the make-believe rain would come pouring down and Daddy would fling up the covers and scooch in beside Matt. They'd finish their picnic all covered up. Then do it again. Ten minutes, tops.

Suggest that he take your child with him when he can — to work, on trips, on errands. Excursions like errands are a great time for dads and their children to relax around one another. And it gives children a better understanding of what it means to be a man, a provider, someone who takes care of things.

I remember going to my dad's office on the weekends — so clearly, in fact, I can still hear his footsteps in the empty hallway from forty years ago. I loved seeing his name on his door and fiddling with all the office stuff that entrances kids. It remains part of my picture of him.

Traveling is a great bonder. As a young boy, our son Matt had quite an itinerary. Ron traveled frequently then, and I encouraged him to take our son along when Matt was old enough. Those long flights together created memories that are theirs alone, and encouraged a communication that has deepened over the years.

Make it easy for him to admit his mistakes and apologize when he needs to. This is a hard one. The best way to encourage apologies is to demonstrate them — or at least tell him about yours in detail when you can. He'll feel awkward apologizing at first (as we all do), but it will develop a closeness between him and your children, provide an example of how they should behave, and be a model of humility and godly living that your children will never forget.

Let him do the dad things without intervening (unless absolutely necessary). The times Ron has taken our children whitewater rafting or rock climbing,

I've chosen to stay away. When I'm not along, my kids can take risks that I should, but might not, permit.

One time Ron and Matt were climbing the wet, slippery rocks behind a waterfall. Matt was above Ron, moving at a teenage clip, when Ron heard him scream. Instinctively, my husband shot his arm straight out just in time for Matt to straddle it and break his fall.

As hard as it is for me to let Ron and our kids do potentially dangerous things, I know it's important for all of them. I'm glad Matt and Molly have a parent who'll do those crazy stunts with them. And I'm even gladder it's not me.

Upstream from Here

What kind of a dad is your husband? Is he throwing a football in the living room with your nine-year-old or parked in front of the football game? Has he taught your daughter how to tie her shoes or how not to throw like a girl? Whatever he's like, your man is the other half of those chopsticks. He's the other current in the stream. And together you can be parents of promise.

Remember my parasailing adventure? Before I ever put on my first para-sail harness, I watched our eleven-year-old son soar into the air. He was so light he flew high above the other parachutes until I could barely see his slight body in the sky. Even now, it makes me shudder to think of it. Quietly shaking with tears, I stood with my camera trained on him, convinced that if I blinked I'd lose sight of him.

It was one of those cut-the-strings experiences. "Let him go, let him go," Ron urged, whispering between my sobs.

In our house, the father encourages the brave things, the mother checks the harnesses. Maybe in your home, you're the adventurous one, and he's checking the ropes. That's all right. God put you together. He knows the right combination — and, by the way, He's even got His eye on those young teenage boys driving that boat.

Promising Conversations

Psalm 127:3–5 — *"Behold, children are a gift of the Lord; The fruit of the womb is a reward. Like arrows in the hand of a warrior, so are the children of one's youth. How blessed is the man whose quiver is full of them."*

1. In what ways have you seen your husband's growth impact your family?

2. Review this suggested list of ways to help your husband be involved with his children, with room for your own suggestions. How can you practically implement these things?
   - Remind him of special occasions (helpful vs. bossy tone).
   - Affirm him in front of the kids.
   - Give him hints on the best ways to spend time with his children.
   - Appreciate it when he admits his mistakes and apologizes.
   -
   -

3. Choose an area to work on this week, and give your group permission to hold you accountable for it.

Private Considerations

1. Write down your parenting goals, along with what you think your husband's goals are. How different are they really?

2. Do you have any unrealistic expectations of your husband as a father? What are they, if any?

3. How would your husband say that you help him to be a good dad? How about asking him how you can better support this area of his life?

Perhaps it is no wonder that the women were first at the Cradle and last at the Cross. They had never known a man like this Man — there never has been such another. A prophet and teacher who never nagged at them, never flattered or coaxed or patronized; who never made arch jokes about them, never treated them either as "The women, God help us!" or "The ladies, God bless them!"; who rebuked without querulousness and praised without condescension; who took their questions and arguments seriously; who never mapped out their sphere for them, never urged them to be feminine or jeered at them for being female, who had no axe to grind and no uneasy male dignity to defend; who took them as he found them and was completely unself-conscious.

DOROTHY SAYERS

A Woman's Turn to Promise

Imagine it's your wedding day. For two tumultuous years you waited for the man you love to propose. Now the time has come, and your wedding is planned for a Saturday morning on a grassy bluff overlooking the ocean. You've heard "warm and clear" from your new friend the weatherman, whose number you know by heart. Thank goodness it's all working out.

Oh, what a beautiful morning. Puffy white clouds that look like foam from your morning cappuccino dot a sky as blue as his eyes. A tiny breeze stirs your veil; the seagulls cackle over the beach but thankfully not over your preparations; and it's a really good hair day. Your nails and makeup are perfect. Your handsome fiancé grudgingly but gracefully wore a black tux instead of jeans and a white T-shirt. He looks magnificent.

Down at the bottom of the hill you stand in your billowing wedding gown (white if you're a "winter," off-white if you're a "fall"). The skirt's so big your waist looks like it belongs to your twelve-year-old sister who's watching every move you make through adoring, envious eyes. No runs in your pat-terned, white stockings, no scuffs on your satin shoes.

You've prayed through every aspect of this day — but you forgot to pray away the rain from the night before, which was relentless enough to mess things up. The grass is sloggy; there are actual puddles in front of you. How will you get up that hill to the arms of your Prince Charming?

No matter how eager you are, it will take some thoughtful planning to get there in as fine a shape as you started. If it weren't for the railroad ties buried here and there, planks to stabilize your path, you'd have no clean way of getting to your man. You gather up your skirts and make your way up the hill. Your head's down, your eyes are on your next step. Slowly you tiptoe from tie to tie, keeping your skirt and train high in the air to avoid the water and mud.

It's this same kind of careful approach and determination that protects us as we try to skirt all the obstacles that appear in the paths of marriage. It takes work to walk that carefully. Each plank could be compared to promises we make, commitments we stand on to stay on track in our marriages and in our own lives. They're the same sort of planks our husbands are standing on as they're promising commitment to God, to their families, and to their friends.

We've looked at some of the obstacles men encounter on their walk up the hill. All along we've talked about how you can cheer on the changes. But it's vitally important also to talk about *your* need to grow. Part of this might include composing some promises of your own.

Often we're so bound to our families, so busy supporting them, or so focused on our husbands, we can't find our own purposes, our own unique course. But as my friend Heather says, "You are not your marriage."

So what kind of promises might a woman make — for herself, others, and God? What kind of woman might she emulate? How about a woman both ordinary and extraordinary? How about one who, similar to us, had to deal with a husband, children, heartbreak, happiness, and disappointment?

"Do you, Mary…"

There are many, many godly women from the beginning of time worthy of emulation. You probably have several in your church. But for the sake of illustration, let's identify with a familiar young woman who "found favor with God."

Mary, Jesus' mother, was an ordinary young woman chosen for an extraordinary relationship. "She was entirely unique in her role as the biological mother of our Lord," says Jack Hayford in *The Mary Miracle*, "but God's Word also shows she was entirely the same as we are in virtually every other way — as a subject of God's grace, as a person needing comfort and assurance, and as a worshiper amazed at God's greatness being shown to her."[1]

Mary was called "favored one." Her response to God's invitation to be involved in His extraordinary plot showed such courage, such integrity and character. Most likely you and I will not have a conversation with Gabriel in which God gives us such a weighty assignment.

But like Mary we ordinary women *are* chosen for extraordinary relationships. We're partners in promise as she was. With God. With our families. Mary's response to God's intervention in her life can be a pattern for our promises — the planks we need for getting up that hill without losing a shoe. What I've written may not express your thoughts exactly. But hopefully, it will help you think about the changes and promises you want to make to keep growing as a human being and as a woman.

1. I promise to believe what God says about me. Most likely, Mary was a teenager working around her mother's house when Gabriel showed up. She was betrothed to Joseph, but we don't even know if she liked him! Or he her, for that matter. He did want to "divorce" her when he first heard about her pregnancy. Mary was going to be pregnant by the Holy Spirit outside of marriage? Who'd be crazy enough to believe that? From a human perspective she was in a very precarious position. But Gabriel called her a "woman richly blessed" and assured her that she had "found favor with God."

That greeting certainly got Mary's attention. "She was greatly troubled at this statement, and kept pondering what kind of salutation this might be" (Luke 1:29). To have God speak to a Jewish girl and elevate her to this favored position was unthinkable. But Mary accepted God's evaluation of her. How could she not? He said it.

Part of the miracle of the conception of Jesus was that this young woman would receive the blessing of God on her gender, her youth, her obedience. And that she would believe it.

God wants to start working with us in the same place — believing our own miraculous conception, our own favored status. When we can picture ourselves being as favored as Mary was, we can finally accept the fact that God does love us and wants to be intimately involved in our lives.

Ask yourself, "Do I know God's opinion of His creation — me? Do I believe He's concerned with what and who I am?" Then read Psalm 139 to see how well acquainted with you He is.

2. *I promise not to turn away from God's plan.* Mary was frightened by Gabriel's report of God's plan, but she didn't turn away. What a shock it must have been for her to suddenly see an angel before her. And then to hear his pronouncements for her life — a pregnancy when she hadn't slept with a man, a son who "will be great, and will be called the Son of the Most High." And to hear about God's favor toward her.

All those things must have made her young mind spin. But Mary knew that God would be involved from start to finish; it wasn't her show alone. That made it possible for her to say, "Be it done to me according to your word" (Luke 1:38).

Our challenge is to develop the kind of relationship with God that makes it possible for us to say those same words. If we know God well enough, we can trust His character in every situation He brings into our lives. That knowledge of God gives us courage because we can trust that He doesn't make mistakes and that He gives us only what we can handle.

When we "hear" God's plan for us, in our Bible reading, in our prayer time, in counsel from other Christians, we have a choice to make just as Mary did. His plan may be a challenging one. But when we know God's working and that He's carefully orchestrated that plan, even though it may be a little scary, we can't turn away. What we can count on is that God's plan is His invitation to obedience on our part, and a guarantee on His part that He'll go with us.

God's plan brings with it a promise of His involvement.

Ask yourself, "Am I willing to stick with what God's doing in my marriage? Do I know Him well enough to trust that He's planned all this and that He guarantees He'll be part of it all the way?" Read Romans 8 to see a small picture of His plan, His character, and His love. And memorize Philippians 4:13 as a reminder that with Christ we're capable.

3. *I promise to be honest with God.* Gabriel reported the fulfillment of prophecy to Mary in Luke 1:32–33. Being Jewish and of King David's line, Mary had undoubtedly heard the messianic prophecy throughout her childhood. Still, Gabriel was telling her amazing things — things that would bring enormous questions from her parents and friends and from the local rabbis.

But Mary's question didn't concern the earth-shattering events to come. It was much more practical and personal. It had to do with the pregnancy, probably stemming from the stigma an unmarried pregnant girl bore. So she asked it. "How can this be, since I am a virgin" (Luke 1:34)?

And that's the question God answered through Gabriel. He told her, "The Holy Spirit will come upon you, and the power of the Most High will overshadow you" (Luke 1:35).

God wants the same kind of interchange with us. We won't always get as clear an answer as Mary did with Gabriel right in front of her, but that doesn't mean the answers aren't there. He is ready for our questions. He's prepared to be pelted with them. He doesn't get tired, weary, bothered, or annoyed when we are honest with our fears and feelings, even if our questions aren't dealing with the biggest issues at hand. What's important to us is important to Him.

He's the only one we can bug with our concerns. He's the only one we can talk to without reservation about our husbands, our marriages, our sex lives, our children.

Develop an ongoing, on-growing, prayer life — both concentrated prayer times in a quiet place and continuous prayer you can use throughout the day.

Ask yourself, "Do I know how to pray? Do I know what to tell God about and ask Him for? Have I been honest with Him about how I feel, about my sin, about my doubts and fears?" Then read Psalm 86, John 16:23–27, and Philippians 4 to find out how eager God is to hear your voice — and anything and everything you have to say.

4. I promise to stick close to my husband through change and let him become what God wants him to be. We don't know much about Mary and Joseph's relationship. He actually was the one who stuck with *her* when things took a different turn. The underlying principle is that God has brought all this about, for Mary and Joseph, and for us and our husbands. When we stick close to the person we've married, we're agreeing with God that His plan has merit. Even when change is painful, slight, intermittent, or huge, it's part of the design for our lives.

We do know that Mary stayed with her husband and Son even though those relationships cost her. She obeyed by playing out her role in this drama. We, too, have a role in our husbands' changes. Part of that role is just sticking with it — and them.

It's a noble thing to hang in there with another person, demonstrating a belief that the future is promising, that potential is forthcoming, that we have enough staying power to make it to the end. How encouraging to communicate to another person that he's worth our while!

When I look at the families represented in this book, I see men and women who are living out that belief in one another through extremely hard times. It's not a belief that ignores the difficulties. It's a belief that gets you through them.

And it's a belief that God's plan has merit. Letting others go through their own growth process is not so hard when God has the proper place in our lives.

Ask yourself, "Am I willing to be the support I need to be to encourage the growth of my husband? Do I know how to live a Christlike life in front of him? Can God give me the strength to do the right thing, even if it means occasionally putting myself aside?" Then read Romans 12 and 1 Corinthians 13 to see what daily Christian living looks like.

5. *I promise to enlist help in keeping these promises.* Mary reached out to a friend in a similar situation as soon as possible. "And behold," Gabriel said, "even your relative Elizabeth has also conceived a son in her old age...for nothing will be impossible with God" (Luke 1:36–37).

Shortly after the angel's visit, Mary went to see the other woman with the "miraculous" pregnancy, her aunt Elizabeth. She needed another woman to confide in, to share with, who'd believe her story, and who had one of her own.

I love this part. Mary was in a unique situation. How wonderful of God to give Elizabeth to her. What a comfort that must have been. Even though Elizabeth was not bearing the Son of God, her pregnancy was still a miracle, as she had been barren up to that point "in her old age." When her baby leapt in her womb at Mary's arrival, it further confirmed what God was doing.

One of the remarkable ways God works in our lives is to supply us with friends who can share our foxholes. Through them we gain courage and insight. We expand our understanding of God and man. We learn by observation and conversation. There are so many passages in the Bible that deal with relationships between believers. It's obvious that we're to have friends at all levels of communication.

Ask yourself, "Do I know anyone who can be in an accountable relationship with me? Do I know how to be that kind of friend?" And then read the story of Jonathan and David in 1 Samuel 18–20.

6. *I promise to keep growing and learning myself.* It's a great thing for a woman, for any person, to continue to grow as much and as long as possible. Can you imagine what it must have been like for Mary to raise her Son, then follow and learn from Him? To move from mom to disciple? For His role to switch from child to Teacher? No doubt from the moment He could talk, He taught her things about living, and she never stopped learning.

We can keep our minds stimulated by reading, risking, tackling new projects, and trying new ways of doing old things. It's good for our families for us to develop some area of our lives. It makes sense to learn more about situations we're in and about interests we have.

Even when family obligations push time for ourselves away, make some time to grow in an area. Schedule an hour for reading; sign up for a seminar; attend a Bible study that will push you; take a computer class; learn how to change a tire; go to the symphony; take line-dancing lessons!

One year when my children were taking piano lessons, I found out that their teacher could give me cello lessons as well. So I rented a cello, one of my favorite instruments, and began to learn to play. A year or two later, when Molly played violin in fifth grade, I went along with my cello and provided some bass notes for the mainly violin orchestra. I was absolutely terrible. But I knew just enough, and had enough pride, to get by and fake everyone out. I had a lot of fun — and haven't played since.

Ask yourself, "What things would I be doing or learning if I didn't have a husband or family? Does anything make me pound the table in anger or frustration that I want to get involved in? Where do I need to grow as a wife or mother, and what can I do to see that growth?" Then read Proverbs 31 with new eyes. Look at all the things she could do. And remember she didn't do them all on Tuesday.

7. *I promise to put my family's best first.* Mary didn't have a choice between being a lawyer or being a mother. If we're wives and moms, none of us has a choice. We may choose where we spend the bulk of our time, but a wife is a wife and a mom is a mom. Mary's choice, and ours, wasn't between careers but between obedience with a joyful heart or disobedience.

That's where our first decision lies. Like Mary, the situations God brings into our laps, in the persons of our husbands and children (if we have them), dictate the first of God's callings for us. It's where we choose between rights and responsibilities. Putting other people first is a sign of character not compromise. And strangely enough, when we do that we elevate our position as wife, mother, and friend.

Putting our families first doesn't mean we ignore the basic needs we face as women. It means that we continually evaluate and adjust, recognizing that sometimes we err by allowing our wants to become needs. Often our self-sacrifice will be the model that motivates our family members and friends to do the same. However, putting others first doesn't mean we cater to their every whim. Sometimes it's harder, more of a sacrifice, to say, "You fix it yourself."

Women are in a unique role. We have the opportunity to show the world what sacrificial living is all about. Ask yourself, "Do I understand what it means to be a Christ-centered wife and mother? Do I have values that reflect Scripture or the world?" Then read Proverbs 1, Philippians 2:1–4, and Titus 2.

A Time of One's Own

I urge you to schedule at least half a day away from your home and family soon. Take an inventory of your roles as a child of God, as a wife, as a mother (if that fits), as a friend, as a human being. Go through the promises above

— and make a few of your own. So much of what we struggle with is only a struggle because we don't take the time to examine the problem and come up with the solution.

When we had small children, Ron agreed that I needed an occasional weekend away. The very first time I did this, I went by myself for two nights to a little hotel about ten minutes from my house. For the first several hours I talked to myself. I'd walk around the room muttering, "And now I'm going to sit down in this chair."

Everything I did and every move I made I made s-l-o-w-l-y. I was on no one's timetable but my own. I gave myself a manicure and a pedicure. I took a nap and watched TV (no competition for the remote). I took a long, luxurious bath. *No one*, I repeat, *no one* asked me what I was doing in the bathroom or how soon I'd feed him. I hardly knew what to do with myself.

The getting-started question I ask myself on these weekends is, what do I want to 'look' like when I'm seventy years old? I ask that question regarding several areas: physical, mental, spiritual, and relational. Then I break them down into more specific sections. Under physical, I consider weight, exercise, diet, sleeping habits. Under mental, I might list books I want to read, subjects I want to understand or explore, issues I want to be able to discuss or defend.

At some point, I consider my weaknesses, like cooking and organization; my "projects in procrastination," like photo albums and closets; my "I shoulds," such as correspondence.

After the fun part of thinking through these areas, I bring all the dreaming back to reality and set some five-year goals with this question in mind: "If I want to be such-and-such when I'm seventy, in the next five years I'll need to do what?" Then those five-year goals need to be brought down to one-year goals and then shorter ones.

It's not often that people use what looks like a business plan to direct their personal lives. It's a shame, because it works. Planning and scheduling help us put feet to our fantasies, skin on the bones of our dreams. We all know what happens when we don't plan — not nearly as much as we would have liked.

Marriage is a blending of two egos, two personalities, two "ways of doing things." The adventure is learning to do it with artfulness, style, compassion, grace, understanding, integrity, and honor. Being the other chopstick does take sacrifice on our part, and on our husband's part as well. But listen to what Barbara Rainey has concluded:

> Through the years, as I have tried to fulfill my role as wife, I have struggled at times with the feeling that my desires and dreams were getting lost in the shuffle. Adapting to, respecting, and even understanding my husband has been difficult on many occasions. Sometimes the sacrifice seemed too great. In these instances, I felt as if God were leading me where I hadn't chosen to go and where I was not skilled.
>
> During those times, the following beliefs have enabled me to maintain a positive perspective and to see my situation more clearly:
>
> 1. I believe firmly in God's sovereignty and am sure of His loving direction for my life.
>
> 2. I believe that God sovereignly led me to marriage. As a result, I have chosen to submit my life, not only to God's authority but to my husband's as well.
>
> 3. I am convinced that God is still sovereignly leading me through my marriage, just as much as He did when I was single. God's will for me is not hampered by my married state.

4. Although much of God's will for me is a consequence of His will for Dennis, I believe I'm not a tagalong or an appendage. We are partners; we are one. God's will for him is God's will for me.[2]

Barbara is right on target. God can enrich, direct, and satisfy your life when you choose to be a partner in promise. He's made you a strong woman with convictions and abilities, and he's linked you up with a man who needs your strength and support.

It's a great adventure — being in the center of God's will. But adventures include marshes to wade through and mountains to climb. As you go forward, you can find strength in His grace. The promises you make will honor Him, as well as each other. And together, as partners in promise, you'll have amazing things to offer the world.

Promising Conversations

> Philippians 3:13–14—*"Brethren, I do not regard myself as having laid hold of it yet; but one thing I do: forgetting what lies behind and reaching forward to what lies ahead. I press on toward the goal for the prize of the upward call of God in Christ Jesus."*

1. What's the biggest change in your own personal growth since you started this book?

2. How might you redefine biblical marriage in light of these past weeks of discussion?

3. In what ways do you have a hard time putting your family's best first? Do you think this is a "fair" philosophy to follow? Why or why not?

Private Considerations

Read Proverbs 31:10–31, as if for the first time. Notice that this woman's activities give us permission to develop and use our gifts and abilities with only two conditions: that we do our husbands good and not evil so they can trust us (vv. 11–12), and that we fear the Lord (vs. 30).

1. What do you want to "look like" at age seventy? Write out a description of your anticipated character, contribution, and family.

2. What steps can you take in the next six months that will start you on your way?

3. What have you always dreamed of doing, but never tried? Is it time?

A N   I N V I T A T I O N

Have you come to the end of this book wondering what I mean when I talk about trusting God? Wondering how you can have a personal relationship with Him? Or what is a Christian, really?

Becoming a Christian is somewhat like sitting in a chair. I can believe a chair will hold me, but until I actually sit in it, I'm not really trusting it to support me. The same is true about coming into a relationship with God through His Son. I can believe that Jesus died for my sins, but until I actually accept Him into my life, I'm not really trusting His payment for my sin.

"Sitting in that chair" is where the power comes from — the power to stick with tough situations, the power to respond not react, the power to love the unlovely. When God's power resides in us, because of our acceptance of Jesus as our Savior, we have a supernatural resource to tap.

According to 1 John 5:11–12, Jesus is the one sure thing we need to secure eternal life and a daily relationship with God. "And the witness is this, that God has given us eternal life, and this life is in His Son. He who has the Son has the life; he who does not have the Son of God does not have the [eternal] life."

Are you ready to take a step toward a God who loves you so much that He sent His only son to die *just for you?* A simple prayer is all it takes, one like I prayed in college, in 1968. It went something like this:

Dear Father, I need You. Thank You for sending Your son, Jesus, to die on the cross for me, forgiving my sins. Come into my life and make me into the person you want me to be. Thank you for hearing my prayer and giving me eternal life. Amen.

A prayer like that marked the beginning of my Christian life. "Christian" means "Christ in one." Once you ask Jesus to come into your life, He will actually live inside you (Romans 10:9; Revelation 3:20). His presence gives us unlimited fellowship with His Father. And that's how our relationship with God begins.

I'm learning daily what it means to have an intimate relationship with God; I'm learning daily to pray through all sorts of situations in my life; I'm experiencing daily what it's like to go through difficult times with joy. There's really nothing like it.

Chapter One: Behold the Stadium

1. You can contact Connie Schaedel at Promise Reapers, P. O. Box 924887, Houston, TX 77292.

Chapter Three: From Where a Wife Stands

1. Nancy Swihart and Ken Canfield, *Beside Every Great Dad* (Wheaton, Ill.: Tyndale House Publishers, Inc., 1993), 241.

Chapter Four: Change Has a Way

1. Nancy Schlossberg, "Taking the Mystery Out of Change," *Psychology Today*, May 1987, 74.

2. Susan Jacoby, "Meeting the Challenge of Change," *Cosmopolitan*, April 1989, 272–74

3. Warren Farrell, *Why Men Are the Way They Are* (New York: Berkley Books, 1986), 322.

4. Ibid., 313.

Chapter Five: The Same Old Guy

1. As quoted by Susan Squire, "Does Your Heart Still Belong to Daddy?" *Cosmopolitan*, January 1992, 118–22.

2. Robert Hicks, *Uneasy Manhood: The Quest for Self-Understanding* (Nashville: Thomas Nelson Publishers, Oliver Nelson, 1991), 30–31.

3. Ibid., 176–77.

4. Ibid., 178.

5. Elisabeth Elliot, *Let Me Be a Woman* (Wheaton, Ill.: Tyndale House Publishers, 1976), 97.

Chapter Six: Who's Leading Whom?

1. Karen Levine, "Are Dads Doing More?" *Parents Magazine*, June 1989.

2. Glen Norval, *Psychology Today*, October 1987.

3. Dennis and Barbara Rainey, *The New Building Your Mate's Self-Esteem* (Nashville: Thomas Nelson Publishers, 1995), 269–70.

4. Ibid.

Chapter Seven: Choices of the Heart

1. Neil T. Anderson, *The Bondage Breaker* (Eugene, Ore.: Harvest House Publishers, 1990), 195, 197.
2. Swihart and Canfield, *Beside Every Great Dad*, 243.
3. Ibid., 237.
4. Hicks, *Uneasy Manhood*, 25.
5. Elliot, *Let Me Be a Woman*, 96.
6. Dennis and Barbara Rainey, *Building Your Mate's Self-Esteem* (San Bernardino, Calif.: Here's Life Publishers, 1986), 80.

Chapter Eight: Love Covers a Lot of Stuff

1. Gary Chapman, *The Five Love Languages: How to Express Heartfelt Commitment to Your Mate* (Chicago: Northfield Publishing, 1992, 1995).
2. Swihart and Canfield, *Beside Every Great Dad*, 173.
3. *Focus on the Family Newsletter*, February 1995.

Chapter Nine: God Is Greater

1. Hicks, *Uneasy Manhood*, 193–94.

Chapter Ten: Friends Need Friends

1. Ron Jenson, *Make a Life, Not Just a Living* (Nashville: Thomas Nelson Publishers, 1995), 132–33.
2. Howard and William Hendricks, *As Iron Sharpens Iron* (Chicago: Moody Press, 1995), 31.

Chapter Eleven: Partners in Parenting

1. "Fathering in America," *Today's Father*, vol. 3, no. 2–3.

Chapter Twelve: A Woman's Turn to Promise

1. Jack Hayford, *The Mary Miracle* (Ventura, Calif.: Gospel Light, Regal Books, 1994), 60.
2. Rainey, *The New Build Your Mate's Self-Esteem*, 269–70.

1   9 4 6 1